MW01179091

Our Lives in Our Hands

Our Lives in Our Hands

Micmac Indian Basketmakers

Bunny McBride

Photographs by Donald Sanipass

NIMBUS
PUBLISHING

Nimbus Publishing Limited
P.O. Box 9301, Station A
Halifax, Nova Scotia
B3K 5N5

Our Lives in Our Hands is partially funded by grants from
the Maine Community Foundation and the Maine Arts
Commission.

Cover photograph of Harold Lafford by R. Todd Hoffman

Canadian Cataloguing in Publication Data

McBride, Bunny.
    Our lives in our hands
    ISBN 0-921054-82-3
1. Micmac Indians — Basket making. 2. Indians of
North America — Maritime Provinces — Basket
making. I. Sanipass, Donald II. Title.
E99.M6M32 1991   971.5'004973   C91-097524-8

Contents

To Micmac hands of the future—
may they be well used.

Foreword

This book is an outgrowth of a tribal project to gather a permanent museum-quality collection, including photographic and written biographical documentation, of the work of today's Aroostook County Micmac basketmakers. Named after a documentary film about Micmac basketry,[1] it represents a desire among our Micmac elders to keep the craft alive and to preserve samples of this vital piece of Micmac tradition for future generations.

Until this project, contemporary Micmac basketmakers in the Aroostook Band, even though they represent the tail end of many generations of Indian basketmakers, had not managed to hold on to a single basket representing the work of our ancestors. The reason is simple: Micmacs have traditionally produced baskets not for the sake of art and posterity but out of economic necessity. For the last two hundred years, our people have relied on basket sales to supplement the small seasonal wages they have earned as migrant farm-laborers, lumberjacks, and domestics. Baskets were crafted for immediate sale and often made the difference between feeding or not feeding one's family. In fact, until the mid-1960s, Micmac basketmakers were often paid for their wares with food. As basketmaker Sarah Lund puts it, "We made baskets because choices were few and we had to eat. If I needed flour or baking powder, I'd make a half dozen baskets, go to the store, and trade them for as many groceries as the store owner said they were worth."

So it was that countless artifacts representing our tribal heritage slipped through Micmac fingers generation after generation. Increasingly concerned about this cultural drain, Micmac elders in the Aroostook Band asked our tribal council to seek funding to preserve sample works and tools of present-day basketmakers who are members of the band. To our great pleasure, the Maine Community Foundation in Ellsworth provided a grant for the collection, as well as for photographic and written documentation. These provided the foundation for this book.

The Aroostook Band is one of twenty-nine bands belonging to the Micmac Nation which traditionally inhabits northeast North America (the Canadian Maritimes, Quebec, Newfoundland, and Maine). Although this book profiles contemporary basketmakers from one particular band, it reveals much about the lives of all Micmacs, as well as our neighboring tribes, the Penobscot, Passamaquoddy, and Maliseet.

Today, as in past centuries, Micmac residency is determined primarily by economic circumstances rather than international boundaries. In fact, the Jay Treaty of 1794 secures our native right to freely cross the U.S.–Canadian border to work in both countries.

The result is that fellow tribespeople who are members of other bands frequent Aroostook County. Among these is Jimmy Labobe, a fine basketmaker who can often be found working with local Micmac artisans in the County.

In addition to regular passersby like Jimmy and the artisans whose lives are highlighted in these pages, we wish to pay tribute to Aroostook Micmac basketmakers who died in recent years, especially Frank Paul and Henry Lafford. Also of special note to our band are emerging basketmakers Yvonne Nadeau, Alex Harquail, Frank Hanning, and Roberta Hanning Murray, as well as established basketmakers Betsy Paul Larke, Marline Sanipass, and Sherman Peters, who have moved out of Aroostook for the time being.

The photographs of the craftspeople included in this book offer an insider's look at basketry; they were taken by our former band president Donald Sanipass, one of the ablest basketmakers in Maine. Hallowell photographer David Spahr did the studio shots of the collection, plus all lab work. Bunny McBride, who has served our band as researcher and advisor for nearly a decade, interviewed the craftspeople and wrote their biographies. She, along with our staff anthropologist, Harald Prins, authored the opening historical essay which provides a long-term perspective on basketry and Micmac life. Major funding for this book and for exhibitions of the basketry collection and photographs came from the Maine Arts Commission.

On behalf of the entire Micmac community, I extend sincere thanks to everyone who participated in this project. It means the preservation of the pride, dignity, and crafts-manship of past, present, and future Micmac craftspeople.

Mary Philbrook, President
Aroostook Micmac Council
August, 1990

Introductory Essay

Today, it is difficult, if not impossible, to find a Micmac Indian in Aroostook County who is over forty years old and didn't grow up in a family that put their hands to wood splint basketry at least seasonally. This is partly because Aroostook has been potato country for more than a century, and until the 1960s the entire crop was handpicked using wood splint baskets made by Native Americans in the region. Micmacs, along with Maliseets, Passamaquoddies, and Penobscots, not only made the picking baskets but supplied a significant portion of the picking force. "Podado diggin'" and basket weaving have long fit in with lumber-jacking, clamming, blueberrying, and other seasonal jobs that have kept Micmac families alive. The story of how Micmacs fell into the migrant laborer role is one that reaches back several centuries. Like the stories of other tribes in the region, it is a saga of native resiliency and adaptation, a tale of native traditions adjusting to white economic demands.

Today's Aroostook County Micmac population numbers about 550. The population of the entire Micmac Nation, divided into twenty-nine bands, is about 14,000. Most still live in their ancestral lands which stretch from Newfound-land through Maine. Archaeological findings suggest that their forebears lived in this region some 12,000 years back. Micmacs, variously referred to as Souriquois, Tarrentines, or Gaspesians, appear in the earliest historic records of this region, along with their Penobscot, Passamaquoddy, and

Birchbark box with pine bottom, rim wrapped with spruce root, and embroidery done with porcupine quills colored with natural dyes. Circa 1830. From Harald Prins' collection. In the course of the nineteenth-century, wood splint basketry replaced traditional quill work as the Micmacs' most demanded trade craft.

Micmacs and Splint Basketry
Tradition, Adaptation, and Survival
by Bunny McBride and Harald Prins

Maliseet neighbors. Speaking closely related Algonkian languages, these four tribal groups are commonly known as the *Wabanaki*—People of the Dawn.

Traditional Life: Micmacs in the Age of Birchbark

The Creator, according to Micmac tradition, was known as *Niskaminou*—Grandfather Sun. After he made the sky and the earth, the tall trees and the flowers, Niskaminou landed in Micmac country and walked along the coast up to the mouth of a river. There, at a pleasant beach, he bent down and molded a man from the sand. He looked twice at what he had made, gave him the breath of life, and stood up. He did not say a word. He bent down again and made a squaw. He got up and said nothing. These were the first people and they were Micmacs. They were red-brown like the earth, tall and strong and warm with the sun's rays.[2]

In former days, Micmacs called themselves *Ulnook*, meaning "humans," and referred to their homeland as *Megumaage*, which probably translates as "Land of Red Earth." When they encountered fellow tribespeople, they greeted each other saying *niqmaq*, a salutation that means "my kin friends." From this term derived the tribal designation of the Micmac.[3]

For thousands of years Micmac tribespeople lived as migratory hunters and gatherers, moving throughout Maine and the Maritimes. Whether trekking on snowshoes and tugging toboggans in the winter or paddling their light birchbark canoes in the summer, they traveled from woodland to seacoast pursuing nature's seasonally shifting storehouses of fish, fruit, and game.

Their annual cycle consisted of thirteen moons generally named for nature's offerings. It began with coastal seal hunting in January. In early February, they returned to the woods to hunt bear, moose, and caribou, as well as beaver and otter. When the fish began to spawn in early spring, Micmac bands camped at their preferred fishing sites to catch smelt, followed by herring, salmon, and sturgeon. When waterfowl and other birds began nesting on the islands, they collected an abundance of eggs. During the summer they usually remained on the coast, where they fished, dug clams, caught lobsters, and hunted birds such as geese and pigeons. In the middle of September, Micmac families moved upriver to catch eels and gather nuts. For the fall hunt, they dispersed into the woods again, chasing moose and trapping beaver. In December they journeyed to the coast to catch tomcod, which spawned under the ice in bays and estuaries. Soon afterwards, it was seal hunting season again and the Micmacs began yet another annual cycle.[4]

Their canoes were typically covered with the unbroken bark of the white birch (*Betula papyrifera*), also known as canoe birch. While the regular Micmac hunting canoe (*akwit'an*) was some ten feet long, sufficient to carry a family of six plus their gear and hunting dogs, the size of their rough-water seagoing canoes may have been as great as twenty-eight feet. Micmacs traveled enormous distances for food, trade, pleasure, or raids, often crossing expansive stretches of open water, including the fifty- to sixty-mile-wide Bay of Fundy. When they moved between southern Nova Scotia and the Maine coast, for instance, elders in the band would send their strongest paddlers ahead in small

Micmac encampment near Halifax, Nova Scotia. Watercolor by Hibbert Newton Binney, circa 1791. From the collection at the Nova Scotia Museum, Halifax. (In addition to birchbark canoes and dwellings, note splint basketmakers in right-hand foreground).

5

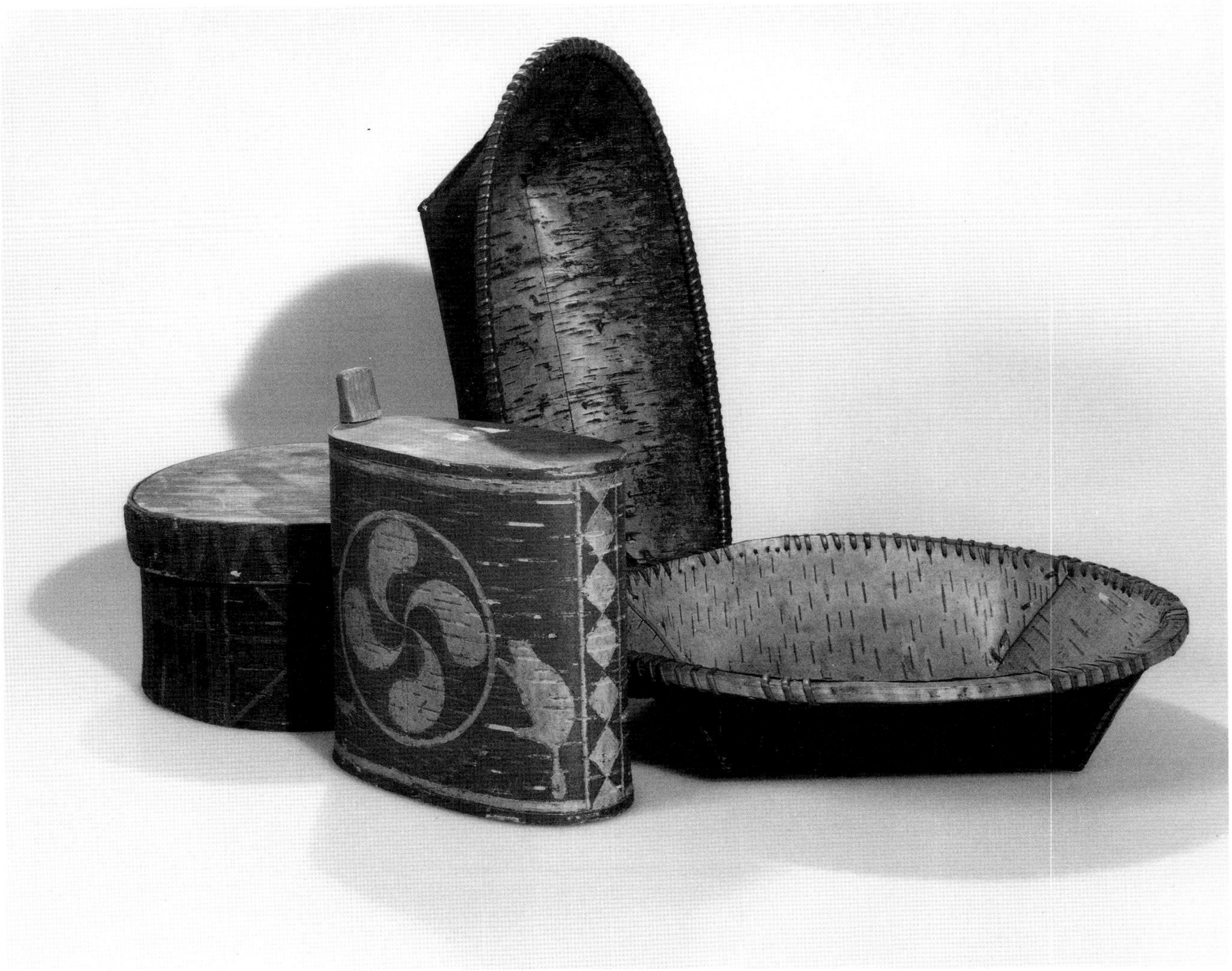

Birchbark utensils: two bowls, an incised storage box, and a gun-powder cannister, also decorated with incised motifs, early twentieth century. From the collection at the Nova Scotia Museum, Halifax.

canoes to the islands lying off the coast. Once there, these vanguard scouts would light beacon fires to direct the other band members following in the larger, slower canoes.[5]

Birchbark, generally called *maskwe*, figured in many aspects of traditional Micmac life. It was used to cover the large conically shaped wigwams in which they lived and to fashion watertight containers of all sizes, as well as special boxes which women embroidered with dyed porcupine quills. Birchbark vessels were usually hung over the fire for cooking meat or were placed directly on coals of hemlock. In addition to birchbark goods, Micmacs constructed a wide variety of woven containers for their own storage, using cattails, sweetgrass, spruce roots, and Indian hemp. These were tucked or hung about the wigwam to hold an array of household supplies such as sewing materials, dried medicinal herbs, carved spoons and ladles, and fibers for weaving bags or braiding ropes.[6]

The following story about the origin of Micmac basketry was told in 1911 by an old Micmac canoe builder named Peter Ginnish of Burnt Church, New Brunswick.

> **A lazy woman was lying down. She rose, scratched the ground, and found a long root. She split it at one end with her teeth; then, holding one end in her teeth, and grasping the other end with her hand, split it lengthwise, into two long fibers. She removed the bark. She did the same with another root. She wrapped the root around her finger several times, leaving eight strands sticking out. The eight pieces served as eight ribs until the basket was finished. No one could name it. It was the first time one had been made, and no one knew what to call it. . . . From that time to the present, baskets have been made; and no one knows how long they will continue to be made. Ai'ip is the name of the woman who first made baskets by twisting roots around her finger. [7]**

Micmacs also fashioned beautiful clothing. Traditionally, men and women dressed similarly in seal or moosehide moccasins, leggings, and a soft leather loincloth attached to a belt at the waist. Over this they wore a smooth leather tunic, usually made of white mooseskin and decorated "in colours of red, violet, and blue, [and] studded with figures of animals, according to the fancy of the work man." These colorful embellishments were made with paint, porcupine quills, and moose hair and were often symbolic representations of guardian spirits, family totems, and other meaningful designs. According to an early visitor who admired their fashions, they even painted their faces "in red or violet, according to fancy, on the nose, over the eyes, and along the cheeks, and they grease the hair with oil to make it shine." In the winter, Micmacs donned warm robes, sewn of beaver or otter furs.[8]

Strangers on the Coast

Micmacs were among the first northeast American Indians to encounter Europeans when they arrived on these shores in the early l500s. Portuguese, Basque, French, and English fishermen, frequenting the nearby Grand Banks, may have ranged the Micmac coast as early as 1504. According to Micmac oral tradition, it was raining when the French first came:

The Indians saw the ship. The children thought the thunder had torn a big tree up. They went home, and said to those there, "See what the storm did last night! . . . The thunder has pitched a big tree up, roots and all."[9]

It is recorded that when two French vessels under command of Jacques Cartier sailed from St. Malo to Chaleur Bay in 1534, the crew was greeted by a fleet of some forty or fifty birchbark canoes manned by Micmac tribesmen. French reports note that the Micmacs "made signs to us to land, holding up skins on the ends of sticks . . . and all drew near our boat, leaping and making signs of gladness and of their wish for friendship, saying in their tongue, *Napeu, ton damen assur tah*, and other words which we understood not." Speaking what appears to have been a Portuguese pidgin, unfamiliar to the French newcomers, these Micmacs invited Cartier to offer trade goods in exchange for their beaver, otter, and other furs.[10]

With the arrival of Europeans in their homeland, Micmac aboriginal culture changed dramatically. In addition to welcomed trade goods such as iron hatchets, knives, needles, arrow-points, fish hooks, copper kettles, woolen blankets, and cloth, the newcomers brought alcohol and deadly diseases which wreaked havoc among the native people. It is estimated that seventy-five to ninety percent of the indigenous population inhabiting the northeast perished due to alien pathogens during the early contact period. These diseases, which included dysentery, measles, smallpox and perhaps most lethal of all, bubonic plague, dramatically reduced the Micmac population to less than two thousand people.[11] In 1611, complaining about the great dying among his fellow Micmacs, an old Micmac chieftain named Membertou recalled that in his younger years Indians had been "as thickly planted there as the hairs upon his head. [But], that they have thus diminished since the French have begun to frequent their country . . ."[12]

The psychological effects of this stunning demise may have contributed to native susceptibility to alcohol abuse. Certainly the liquor available through trade with Europeans quickly became a curse. A local French fur trader frequenting Micmac camps in the course of the seventeenth century reported later that "since they have taken to drinking wine and brandy they are subject to fighting. Their quarreling comes ordinarily from their condition; for being drunk, they say they are all great chiefs, which engenders quarrels between them."[13]

Trappers and Traders

Almost as quickly as the indigenous population declined, the white colonial population grew. With the intricate interdependencies of their traditional lives shattered, native survivors had little choice but to adapt to the new conditions around them. Capitalizing on their subsistence hunting skills, they became specialized fur trappers and market hunters, spending the long winter months trapping and hunting beaver, mink, otter, bear, deer, and moose. Come spring, they canoed to coastal trading posts to exchange their valuable stockpiles of furs for sundry manufactured goods from abroad.

Some Micmac warriors emerged as native middlemen in the transatlantic fur trade. They acquired small European sailing boats, known as shallops, and ranged enormous distances in pursuit of trade. Before French and English fur traders began frequenting coastal Maine on a regular basis, these Micmac entrepreneurs controlled the trade between the Gulf of St. Lawrence and the Maine coast, purchasing furs (especially beaver) for resale.[14] For instance, the captain of an English bark anchored on Maine's southern coast in 1602 reported that he and his crew encountered a small Micmac trading party "in a Basque shallop with mast and sail, an iron grapple, and a kettle of copper." The six tribesmen "came boldly aboard us," he wrote, "one of them appareled with a waistcoat and breeches of black serge, made after our sea-fashion, hose and shoes on his feet. . . . These with a piece of chalk described the coast thereabouts, and could name Placentia [Plaisance] of the Newfoundland . . ."[15]

Historical evidence shows that Micmacs were also trading their crafts from the early colonial period onward, in particular birchbark boxes and pouches decorated with colorful quill mosaics—although these were incidental exchange items compared to furs.[16] Apparently there was no market for their woven containers, for these are never mentioned in the records among the trade goods. As for wood splint baskets, there is no record of Micmacs making them until the latter part of the eighteenth century.

The Scramble for Megumaage

Throughout the colonial era, Micmacs survived by hunting and gathering and by trading furs and crafts. They also survived by making political alliances. When French and English colonials fought over Indian homelands (1613–1763), Micmacs formed a strategic alliance with their French neighbors who supplied them with vital commodities. It was an unsteady existence, influenced by the colonials' erratic demands for military support, sudden epidemics, periodic game depletions, and unpredictable market fluctuations.[17]

In the early seventeenth century, Micmac warriors acquired their first firearms from French traders and were soon feared by their rivals as one of the most powerful native groups in the region. About the same time, French-Catholic missionaries began converting Micmac tribespeople, and Franco-Micmac relations were further strengthened. Reportedly "good hunters, excellent shots with the gun," Micmacs joined neighboring tribes (including the Maliseet, Passamaquoddy, and Penobscot) in the Wabanaki Confederacy later that century. Commenting on their strategic function, a French military observer noted in the l690s that the Micmacs "not only defend their own country and our frontiers, but likewise that they destroy their enemies our neighbors and render it impossible for [the English] to come and establish themselves on our coasts . . ."[18]

During the course of the eighteenth century, the French gradually lost ground and were finally forced out of the region after the fall of Quebec in 1759. With their allies defeated, the Micmacs lost a key survival element and no longer carried political weight in the strategic military or commercial plans of the powerful British nation. This, coupled with a massive invasion of their lands by waves of new immigrants and a general decline in the region's fur trade, reduced the Micmacs to a precarious existence based on subsistence food-collecting and occasional begging.

Taking up the Hatchet

Given these circumstances, it is not surprising that General George Washington's plea for Indian support in the American revolution against British domination received favorable response from Micmac warriors. They promised the American freedom fighters "to stand together and oppose the people of Old England that are endeavouring to take yours and our lands and Libertys from us." During the war, a number of Micmacs, along with other Wabanaki fighters, joined the American forces stationed in Machias. Launching seaborne raids on English shipping and trading posts, many Micmacs were captured or lost their lives, and several tribal villages were destroyed.[19]

When the United States and Great Britain finally signed a peace treaty in Paris in 1783, American authorities showed little consideration for their Micmac and Maliseet allies, who complained that white strangers were taking over their traditional streams and hunting lands. In a formal statement they declared, "We have been fighting for you and secured for America all the lands on this eastward country to the river St. Croix and always been ready to take up the hatchet when you called. You promised to secure for us our hunting grounds. . . . How must we live now, we know nothing but hunting, you white men can live other ways . . ."[20]

Ironically, although the Micmacs had sided with Americans against the British, Micmac reserves were gradually set aside in the Canadian Maritimes by the British government. Yet, many of these reserves were used primarily as way stations or seasonal camps by Micmacs who clung to their traditional migratory lifeways. Ignoring the imposed inter-national boundary lines that the Europeans drew through their lands, Micmacs tried to hold on to fragments of their traditional lives. Moving back and forth across what was now called Canada and the United States, they continued seasonal migrations, mixing subsistence hunting and gathering with selling their crafts and labor to settlers. Often they set up camp near the new settlers.

The Art of Wood Splint Basketry

It is at this point that wood splint basketry enters the historical record in Maine and the Maritimes. Trees such as maple, cedar, spruce, and ash provided Wabanaki Indians with raw materials to weave a variety of baskets desired by settlers for storage and harvest work as well as to hold sewing and knitting supplies and other domestic goods. For the production of sturdy work baskets, Micmacs preferred brown or black ash (*Fraxinus nigra*), due to its unusual flexible strength and durability.[21] This wood, known as *wiskok* and basket ash among Micmacs, grows in swampy areas. Once found, felled, trimmed, and peeled, the trunk is pounded repeatedly with the blunt edge of an ax, which causes it to separate along its annual growth rings into thin layers that can be spliced into strips for weaving. One can either pound the whole log or, like most Micmacs, split a log into long wedges and then pound each section. Micmacs call this pounding process *elikpedaaga* ("to be stripping up wood, or pounding ash, into splints for basket stuff"), and refer to the resultant splints as *likped'gunabe*. The Micmac word for basket, *likpen'igun*, indicates the use of wood-splints as weaving material.[22]

Whether Indians are the originators of splint basketry or

10

got the idea from the infiltrating Europeans is a debated issue. For instance, Micmac artisans profiled in this book say their people have been making splint baskets "since time immemorial." But an old tribal storyteller "with a fund of detailed information about material culture," noted in the early 1900s that such baskets were not made until after the arrival of the whites.[23] Commenting on what may have been a gradual replacement of birchbark by splint basketry, one researcher suggested recently that the craft was introduced by Swedish colonists to Indians in the Delaware Valley about 1700 then diffused its way up to Micmac country in the mid-1800s.[24] Yet, Micmacs had the technological where-withal to make wood splint baskets much earlier—they were thoroughly familiar with the art of splint making prior to the contact period, for they lined their canoes with narrow, quarter-inch-thick white cedar ribs.[25]

Precise timing and invention credits aside, it is clear that Micmacs were doing splint basketry by the late 1700s, for this is depicted on several historic paintings from that period (see p. 5).[26] And by the early 1800s Micmacs were actively responding to the new demands of capitalism by producing splint baskets along with other useful commodities such as ax handles, barrel staves, shingles, and poles for traps and gardens.[27] As there is no firm historical evidence that Micmacs made wood splint baskets earlier for their own use, it appears that they and other native tribespeople in northeast North America produced this basketry expressly to sell to European settlers. And where these crafts were produced directly for sale to white people, it seems that native artisans were influenced in design by the uses for which their customers wanted them.

Settlers appreciated decorative work on some of their household baskets. Toward this end, Micmacs sometimes dyed their splints before weaving or hand painted completed baskets. For color they used local plants. In the following little story, Micmacs explain the origin of dyes:

> **A man was building a canoe, and chewed some of the chips. He spat, and saw that the saliva was black. In this way the people obtained that color. Later they boiled everything to find out what colors various things would produce; and so obtained all their dyes.**[28]

Green, for instance, was distilled from a boiling brew of white cedar twigs and elm bark. Their beautiful vermilion they got from Solomon's seal (*Polygonatum biflorum*), known as eel berry, or from the roots of the lesser bedstraw (*Galium trifidum*), which they also used to dye their porcupine quills. From blueberries they made a reddish pink, while brilliant yellow came from the root of the goldthread (*Coptis trifolia*). In contrast to these naturally harvested dyes, for the color blue they purchased relatively cheap indigo from white storekeepers in the area. Gradually, however, aniline dyes replaced the traditional color sources since they were far easier to use and readily available on the market.[29]

Payment for their wares was meager, sometimes in cash, often in the form of goods such as molasses, flour, sugar, tea, and cloth. Some sold their labor as well as their crafts. Most lived hand-to-mouth, often impoverished, increasingly at the mercy of white settlers who surrounded them in ever-growing numbers.

11

At Doctor Tomah's Camp

To peddle their wares, Micmacs needed to camp, at least periodically, near white settlements. An eyewitness account of a Micmac encampment in the 1840s offers a fascinating detailed sketch of native life at that time. Like so many other nomadic groups, this particular band consisted of about thirty people who usually traveled from place to place by birchbark canoe or sled. It is noted that the band "had twelve large dogs, that did all their teaming, as they could haul a load of twelve hundred pounds easily. . . ." In the fall of 1846, following an elder Micmac herb specialist known as Doctor Tomah, the band set up a temporary winter camp in a grove of rock maples, about ten miles from the nearest white town:

> **We built an excellent camp here, which was forty feet in diameter. We cut first six long spruce poles, and stacked them together in the form of a cone, tying the top ends, and allowing the other ends to be about twenty feet from each other in the form of a circle. Between these poles we placed numerous smaller ones, running both ways, and upon these poles we placed our strips of birchbark, each piece nicely lapping over others, and neatly stitched together with spruce roots. These were tied to the poles, and when thus covered, it was perfectly tight, excepting a hole in the top through which the smoke passed. The fire was built in the middle of the tent, around which when very cold, we would all gather, and pass the time very comfortably.**

While Doctor Tomah gathered medicinal roots and herbs, his sons and others, armed with rifles, hunted or fished. The women picked berries, and made porcupine quill boxes and an assortment of baskets.[30]

Adventurous Marketeers

By this time, Micmacs and other tribespeople in the Northeast were also using public means of transportation, traveling by steamship and train to faraway places for adventure and to find better markets for their wares. For instance, in March, 1847, two young men belonging to Doctor Tomah's Micmac band took the steamer from Halifax to Boston, where they hoped to sell a large number of "fancy quill boxes," for "one to fifteen dollars" apiece. One of their companions, named John Glossian, later recollected:

> **The quill boxes that I carried would pack very snug, one inside of another; so that I had some five or six hundred dollars worth of goods. . . . After arriving there [in Boston], we went off and got us a boarding house, and had things moved to it, and commenced to sell out our stock by standing upon the Common, and selling to passersby, and at other times going from house to house.**
>
> **[Leaving Boston after some time], I stopped at New Bedford a few days, and sold some of my baskets . . . and then went to New York, where I disposed of the balance of my stock. . . . From New York I took the steamer for Halifax, having been gone about two months. I stopped at Halifax, N.S., a few months, and**

12

then as Tomah and his family had a great amount of fancy work, some twenty of us left for New York by steamer, arriving there about the first of August. In New York we hired a tenement, as there were quite a number of us, and leaving the children at home, the older ones went out and sold baskets and boxes. We sold about one-half of our stock while here, and purchasing four horses and two large express wagons, we packed up our goods, and started for Philadelphia, Pennsylvania, camping out as we went along. After arriving there we bought some cloth and made us some tents, and after securing a place, we set them up, and some of us manufactured baskets, while others sold them. This was the first time that I had lived in a cloth tent, and I found it much inferior to the other tents [birchbark wigwams] that I had lived in, for when it rained hard, the water would soak through, making it very uncomfortable. We stopped here about three months, [Tomah practicing medicine, and the other Micmacs] manufacturing and selling baskets, and then we started for Springfield, Mass., camping out upon the sides of the road as we went along.

For at least two years, Doctor Tomah's Micmac band continued to roam the New England countryside, selling medicinal herbs and "making fancy baskets and other small articles." When they set up camp in coastal summer resorts, or at Boston Common, Micmac boys contributed to the collective income of the group, making an "honest penny" from spectators by shooting at coins with their bows and arrows.[31]

With Nimble Fingers

In his 1865 memoirs, Reverend R.J. Uniacke of the Maritimes, commented. . . .

> [The Micmacs] are very ingenious and neat in many kinds of workmanship of wood, [and] thus employ themselves in the manufacture of tubs, buckets, churns, casks, and such utensils, in great quantities which they dispose of to the neighboring inhabitants and settlers. They are very clever at carving in wood, and out of beech they will manufacture very neat spoons, bowls, and troughs for various domestic purposes. Little sleds and bows and arrows for the use of children, also constitute a department of trade with them. Poles and sticks for garden beans and peas are likewise continually brought in by them for sale in the summer time. . . . They come round constantly to the houses, with bundles of materials on their backs,—such as ash for hoops, and will sit down patiently for several hours and mend-up any old buckets or tubs that may be brought to them for repair.[32]

The reverend noted that Micmacs were especially known for their porcupine quill boxes—an ornate and difficult craft which they continued to produce through the early 1900s.

> [Their] bark boxes indeed are famous. These

13

are made of the smooth inner bark of the birch tree, with an inner lining of thin pine wood. The outside is generally covered with a variety of pretty mathematical figures, worked with the quills of the porcupine, which are dyed of the most brilliant colours for this purpose. In bead work also they are remarkably clever, and shew great delicacy of taste; ornamenting bags, belts, and soft caribou-skin moccasins in the most beautiful manner with little glass beads of every colour, which are provided by the merchants, for their express demand.[33]

Changing Culture, Changing Clothes

What did Micmacs look like in the nineteenth century? By the mid–1800s, Micmac men had generally adopted European clothing, sometimes wearing dark blue or black coats modeled after British military greatcoats. Reverend Uniacke described them this way:

They do . . . still partly retain their dress of former years, consisting of a blue tunic, with the seams inlet with scarlet cloth and wings or epaulets upon the shoulders of the same colour. A leather strap once the wampum belt, keeps this tunic close to the waist. A woolen sash of divers colours is sometimes worn. . . . An ordinary round hat covers their head encircled by a coloured band of ribbon. Beads and tin ornaments usually decorate their breast,—and especially their moccasins or shoes, which are made of moose skin and

highly adorned with patterns of bead work. They invariably smoke, and a pouch containing a pipe and tobacco is almost always carried at the waist.

The reverend also left us a written picture of Micmac women:

The dress of the squaw is much more peculiar and striking consisting generally of a coloured bed-gown and loose blanket thrown over the shoulders like a shawl; with petticoats of various colours. The head dress is very peculiar being a high pointed cap of blue or red cloth, with loose ends falling almost over the shoulders,—highly ornamented with bead work of various patterns, and adorned with ribbons.[34]

All Aboard! Trains and Tourists

In the second half of the nineteenth century, the introduction of railways brought ever greater changes into Micmac homelands. The steam locomotive was a mixed blessing for Native Americans in the region. On the one hand, it allowed the international political economy to penetrate even deeper into the "wilderness." On the other hand, it offered the traditionally mobile Micmac a new and efficient mode of transportation which helped them to make a living within the confines of the new economy which now surrounded them. Trains enabled them to travel more conveniently to distant locations for work on river drives or in logging camps. Railways also brought a new kind of intruder into native homelands: the sportsman. Maine, in particular,

14

with its myriad of lakes and streams in vast woodlands, lured holiday hunters who were eager for the thrill of a short-term flirtation with nature. The state quickly gained fame among wealthy sportsmen from New England to the midwest as a rich hunting and fishing area. The intrusion brought with it another modest compensation for native peoples: a new survival option. Micmacs and other Wabanaki Indians hired themselves as guides to the visitors, leading them through the wild interior waterways in birchbark canoes, demonstrating an array of survival skills. For instance, to transport fresh meat from kill-site to hunting camp, Micmac guides fashioned sturdy baskets on location.[35]

In the wake of sporthunters came vacationing "rusticators," urban gentry looking for a respite of simple life and communion with nature. Coastal and lakeside resorts popped up in places like Bar Harbor, Boothbay, and Greenville. By 1872 there were fifteen hotels in Bar Harbor, and Frenchman Bay was replete with the sailing yachts of the upper crust from New York, Boston, and Philadelphia. Such vacationers presented an economic opportunity for Micmacs and other Wabanaki Indians who often traveled by train to set up camp near the resorts each summer to make and peddle crafts, including birchbark boxes and "fancy" splint baskets.

Fancy baskets, yet another adaptation to market demand, were made primarily by Micmac women and catered to the elaborate Victorian taste of the time. Embellished with dyed splints, curlicue splint embroidery, and braided sweetgrass trimming, they were fashioned in many distinct styles to hold hats, gloves, yarn, combs, buttons, sewing goods, handkerchiefs, pies, and picnics. Micmac women also produced various novelty items from splints, such as fans, lamp shades, and flowers. Special hand tools emerged to enhance the precision production of these finer splint baskets—including gauges used to uniformly splice splints. Meanwhile, Micmac men made fishing creels and pack baskets to market among the tourists.[36]

American tourists who ventured to resorts in the Canadian Maritimes were even more likely to encounter Micmacs selling their wares because of the many Micmac reserves there. Caroline Copage, a Micmac born in 1910, remembers that while her father was off working and living in Maine for several years, she and her sister and mother went with her grandparents to set up camp near Charlottetown, Prince Edward Island, each summer: "Grandma used to make mocassins and decorate them with quills and small beads. In the summers, tourists from the U.S. used to come over and buy mocassins from my grandma when we were staying in Rocky Point by Charlottetown. . . . My grandfather used to make birchbark canoes and boxes [to sell], and like most Indians he moved around to make a living."[37]

A Crisis of Supply

By the 1890s the valued white birch—especially the unbroken forty-footer—had became very scarce in Micmac country, primarily due to widespread lumbering activities in the region. In 1894 the last birchbark canoe was made on Indian Island, Pictou County, and one year later the last one was made at Shubenacadie. By then, store-bought canvas had completely replaced bark canoe covers, and permanent frame houses had generally replaced the Micmacs' traditional conical winter dwellings. Soon, Micmac crafts were

Three decorative weaves (l-r): "standard diamond," "porcupine," and "periwinkle." From the collection at the Nova Scotia Museum, Halifax.

also affected by the shortage, which worsened with the spread of an arboreal disease known as birch dieback. Given the dearth of suitable birchbark, Micmacs were also forced to turn to tarpaper to cover their summer wigwams. Finally, in the early 1900s, the birchbark period in Micmac culture effectively came to an end.[38]

Certainly the demise of birchbark artisanry made the economic role of wood splint basketry all the more important among Micmacs and other Wabanaki Indians. The supply of brown ash and other trees used for splint basketry also diminished in the late l800s—but not nearly as extensively as white birch.[39] Although supplies were exhausted on Micmac reserves in Nova Scotia and somewhat scarce in coastal areas, hardy groves of brown ash and cedar could still be found in Aroostook County and interior New Brunswick. Micmacs, adaptive as ever, relocated themselves as necessary to carry on with their lives.

In Maine, as in the Maritimes, very few Wabanaki artisans were named as individuals in written records prior to this century. When mentioned, they were commonly referred to simply as "Indians" or "natives." Among the handful of specifically noted Micmacs in Aroostook County during the nineteenth century are Betsy Bask [Basque] of Monticello, who established herself as basketmaker in the region in 1895. She lived in a rented house and sold her wares to the local public. Three years later, Stephen Dominick and his family, probably from the Miramichi River, set up camp at Gary Plantation, making baskets in the area for many years. In Washington County, records note that a Micmac named Annie Sack made "all kinds" of baskets with her family while her husband and oldest son worked as river drivers and lumberjacks. Although the particular names of early Micmac basketmakers were rarely preserved in Maine's written records, oral history among Micmacs has recorded the exploits of some of these individuals.[40]

After the turn of the century, resorts continued to increase and each summer groups of native artisans continued to set

Since time immemorial, migrating Micmacs have often lived in temporary lodges. This nineteenth-century photo shows a Micmac basketmaking couple in front of their makeshift summer home fashioned of bark. From the collection at the New Brunswick Museum, St. John, N. B., acquisition #72950. Photo by J. S. Climo.

17

up camp near the mountain, lakeside, or coastal retreats most favored by tourists. The demand for their crafts held firm. In fact, during the 1920s the popularity of Micmac baskets became so great that gypsies ventured to Maine resorts with cheap imported baskets and presented themselves as American Indians selling their own handmade goods. In 1930, after repeated complaints from authentic tribespeople, the state ultimately passed a law against impersonating Indians.[41]

The tourist market for novelty baskets transformed entire indigenous communities almost completely into seasonal artisan settlements. Interestingly, Indian villages closest to tourist haunts were by no means homogenous, but represented contingents of basketmakers from various tribal origins. For example, baskets purchased from the Indian Island Penobscot reservation were often the work of Passamaquoddy, Maliseet, Canadian Abenaki, or even Micmac basketmakers residing temporarily in that village. A similar situation existed at the coastal reservation of Pleasant Point, where a few Micmac artisans resided among the local Passamaquoddy Indians.[42]

"Podado" Diggin' in the County

Late nineteenth-century potato farmers, looking for sturdy harvesting containers, vied with tourists for Indian-made baskets. The Maine potato industry took off in 1878, as soon as Aroostook had a rail connection with the outside world. Maine emerged as the country's major potato producer—initially supplying stock for starch production, then leading the way in table stock production.[43] The rugged "Indian potato basket" provided an ideal harvesting tool and has

Potato harvest, New Sweden Road, Caribou, Maine, 1982. Photograph by Katherine Olmstead; reprinted from *Echoes*, Fall, 1988.

18

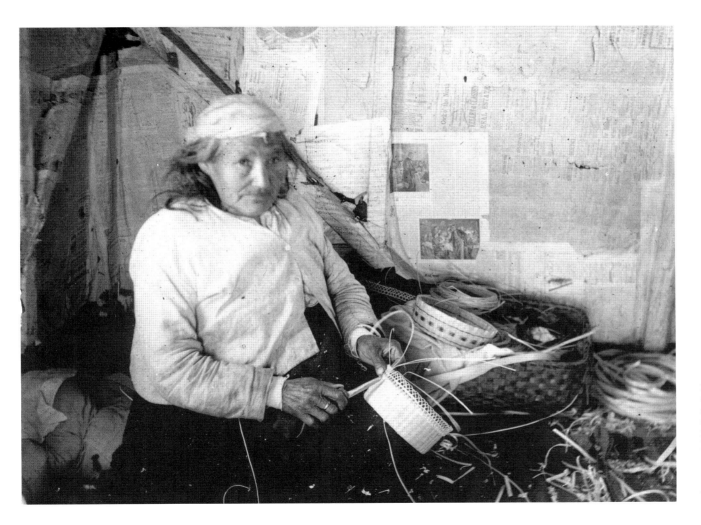

Micmac basketmaker, Queens
County, Nova Scotia, late nineteenth
century. From the collection at the
Queens County Museum, Liverpool,
Nova Scotia. Photo courtesy of the
Nova Scotia Museum, Halifax.

been used to bring in the state's vast crop as far back as anyone can recall. Unfortunately, the origin of this specific splint basket remains a bit of a puzzle. Among farmers in the County it is said that "they originally started picking into bags and those were awkward. In the fall the Indians would come for the harvest. . . . They didn't like the bags. They already had different kinds of baskets and developed one to fit the potato picking job. Musta been about a hundred years ago."[44]

Wabanaki Indians who "hunted ash" and made baskets in the Aroostook area usually participated in the annual potato harvest. Between l920 and 1965 especially, potato picking and basket weaving were integral factors in the migrational seasonal working patterns of thousands of Wabanaki Indians. The heyday of the state's potato industry was mid-twentieth century when acreage peaked at nearly 200,000 and it took nearly 40,000 pickers to bring in the crop.[45] Since each picker had to have a basket, that period was no doubt the heyday of potato basketry as well. Micmac basketmaker Sarah Lund recalls that in those boom days, an Indian family that got a big basket order usually hired other Indians, not always from the same tribe, to help out. "We were all intertwined," says Sarah. "I used to make basket bottoms for a Maliseet family in the l960s. They paid me twenty five cents a bottom to wear out my hands."[46]

During this century, a clear work cycle emerged among Wabanaki Indians which holds to this day for many Micmacs. Echoing their traditional seasonal migrations for hunting/gathering/trading, they moved about as seasonal laborers, digging potatoes in the fall; lumbering in the winter; river driving in the spring; raking blueberries, clam-

Micmac or Maliseet women going to market, circa 1840. Watercolor by John Stanton. From the collection at The New Brunswick Museum, Webster Canadiana Pictorial Collection, #6712.

20

ming, and hawking baskets among farmers and tourists in the summer; and making baskets or working in potato houses whenever there was a labor lull. Sarah, who first picked potatoes in 1933 when she was sixteen, is typical:

> **I went back and forth [between Maine and New Brunswick] for years, following work opportunities and sometimes just following the crazy winds of fate. In June and July I'd be making potato baskets in Aroostook. Then in August I'd go to Washington County picking blueberries. Come September I'd be back up in Aroostook for the potato harvest. After that, if I could find a good rent in Maine, I'd stay here through the winter months. If not, I'd return north. In those cold months we just survived. Come spring, we'd dig clams in Dalhousie, pick fiddleheads in Aroostook. In between it all, I'd work out in people's homes for a dollar a day—cooking, cleaning, looking after things.[47]**

As in the nineteenth century, Micmacs in the twentieth century lived life close to the bone. Unlike former times, when they were free to do as they pleased in a world of natural plenty, they were increasingly confined by the constraints of the modern cash economy. Their artisanry and labor, while needed, even appreciated, rarely offered more than subsistence level living. Living a life of material scarcity, they were likely to define themselves by what they could do with their hands rather than by a batch of possessions or a single address.

In 1950 mechanical harvesters were introduced, and by 1965 only half of Maine's potato crop was still gathered by hand. Since then, a decrease in farm acreage and an ongoing rise in mechanical harvesting have further diminished the traditional farming demand for baskets in Aroostook. Today, less than fifteen percent of the County's potato crop is handpicked using Indian baskets.[48]

The Challenge of Cultural Survival

During the last two decades, the cottage industry of splint basketry has waned among all four tribal groups in Maine. In addition to the decreased demand from farmers, the decline has been spawned by a diminished demand for fancy Victorian-style baskets, the increasing difficulty of finding suitable ash, and the high labor–low cash return nature of the work. Today Maine has fewer than two dozen Native American basketmakers, and about half are Micmac. All are concerned about the diminishing supply of brown ash. It is not simply a problem of over harvesting but one of poor health among existing ash stands. "Something's killing the trees," says Micmac basketmaker Donald Sanipass. "I don't know if it's acid rain or fertilizer runoff from the farms, but the tops of the trees look dead and the wood quality isn't what it used to be."[49]

When today's basketmakers manage to get wood good enough to turn into baskets, they must look far beyond farmers to market their products. Some sell roadside, hawk their baskets shop to shop, or participate in various craft fairs around the state. In 1982 the Aroostook Micmac Council, based in Presque Isle, started a business called the Basket Bank which buys, markets, and distributes Micmac baskets throughout New England. It has gradually devel-

Micmac basketmakers in New Brunswick about 1911. From the collection at the Canadian Museum of Civilization, Ottawa, Ontario.

22

oped a modest market for fancy sewing and jewelry baskets and a more extensive one for a variety of utility baskets (pack, picnic, garden, hamper, and laundry—and the potato basket, which is now sold for everything from home gardening to magazine storage). Encouraged by this, a handful of Micmacs have recently tried to learn or relearn the craft. Richard Silliboy, now forty-three, explains why he didn't take up basketry until recently when the market began to look more hopeful: "Although I came from a basketmaking family, I wasn't interested in it because of the terrible value of baskets in [Aroostook] County. I saw my mother work so hard and get so little out of it. That discouraged me."[50]

Even with the market for some baskets moving in a positive direction, Donald Sanipass admits that the craft is often a grueling, fourteen-hour-a-day business with very modest financial rewards. "It's no picnic being a basketmaker," he concludes. "It's not what you call a good risk thing. But we get by—we keep the wolf man off the door."[51]

Of course it is no picnic or good risk thing raking blueberries, digging potatoes, cutting potato seed, working in damp potato houses, or doing any of the other part-time seasonal jobs that keep so many Micmacs on the move. But the ins and outs and ups and downs of seasonal work have called forth a verve of versatility not uncommon among these people. For centuries they and other Wabanaki Indians have migrated throughout Maine and the Maritimes in search of the best place to make a living at each particular point in time. Generation after generation, Micmac nomadism, ever adapting to changing cultural, economic, and climatic circumstances, has been an intricate, though risky, system of survival. It has enabled the basketmakers profiled in this book, like their ancestors, to resist assimilation and to maintain a measure of their distinct cultural identity while surviving with intermittant scarcity and plenty the repeated revolutionary changes in their options for livelihood. And, according to Sarah Lund, "with all its headaches and uncertainties, there's a special kind of freedom in the basketmaking business. And that's what keeps me going."[52]

Brown ash splints have proven to be as adaptable as Micmacs to the demands of the marketplace—able to be transformed into a big sturdy harvest basket or a delicately detailed sewing basket. The remarkable flexibility of this material, coupled with that of the Micmacs might just save wood splint basketry for the future. But if the brown ash tree is destroyed . . .?

Biographies of Contemporary Micmac Basketmakers in Aroostook County

Sarah Lund and Abe Harquail have been in one another's lives for a long time—nearly five decades. In that time they've produced countless baskets together and traveled great distances to follow seasonal work opportunities. Over the years, they have moved in and out of each other's lives like go-rounds woven between standards: they've been married, separated, divorced, then reunited long enough to be recognized as common-law spouses today. Abe is now eighty and Sarah is sixty-three, and they're still making baskets.

Sarah, the oldest of three girls, was born August 12, 1927, to Peter and Marguerite Bernard Jacobs at Eel River Bar Reserve in New Brunswick. "My parents weren't from Eel River," says Sarah, "but my father had heard baskets were selling good there and that there was a lot of trapping and hunting, so he took my mom there." Marguerite was a full-blooded Micmac, but Peter's family history is vague. "My father was a foundling," says Sarah. "Some claim he was white, but I don't think so—maybe part white, but he was raised by Micmac Indians, and he believed in Indian ways. Dad lived in the woods more than in civilization. He was a great trapper and I've yet to see an Indian equal his basketmaking. . . . He also worked as a hunting guide, often for a fellow named Bill Baker who was a hotel manager in Gaspé, Quebec. Bill had a bunch of guides, including my dad, and Dad sold lots of pack baskets to him."

Peter Jacobs moved about for work and usually took his family with him. When he was out trapping or guiding in Quebec, Marguerite and the girls stayed at a little camp

Abe pulling apart a stick of splints while Sarah weaves a potato basket.

I've been [making baskets] for forty-six years and it's become a habit. You might say it's in my blood. If they opened my veins they'd probably find them full of ash shavings. (S.L.)

Abe Harquail and Sarah Lund
St. John, Maine

deep in the woods of Gaspé. On several occasions they all moved in with Phillip and Nancy Martin who lived on Maria, a Micmac Reserve long known for its many resident basketmakers. "Dad had friends at all the [Micmac] reserves," says Sarah. "He and my mother used to make baskets with Phillip and Nancy. . . . Dad dyed the ash with dyes made of berries, leaves, bark, different grasses, and roots. . . . When they finished a batch, he'd put them on a dog sled and peddle them house to house."

Sarah's mother was often sick, and shortly after her third daughter was born, she died. "At my mother's funeral," recalls Sarah, "I crawled in her casket. I'd always slept with her and I thought it was a fancy bed. My father gave me the worst spanking of my life at that funeral."

In l935, two years after her mother's death, Sarah's father took her to Shubenacadie Indian Residential School in Nova Scotia. During holidays, says Sarah, "My mother's parents used to come from Cambridge Reserve, about fifty miles west, to take me to their home." During those visits Sarah often watched her grandmother, who smoked a clay pipe, making porcupine quillboxes, beaded mocassins and poplar baskets trimmed with seashells.

Seven years after Sarah arrived at "Shubie," her father became sick and she left school to care for him, joining him and her little sisters at the Gaspé camp. Not long afterwards all four of them moved back to Phillip and Nancy's at Maria. "I was fourteen years old and didn't know a thing when I came out of that convent except how to pray," says Sarah. "Nancy taught me the facts of life, and Phillip was so shocked that I couldn't speak Micmac anymore that he refused to speak English to me." (Children were punished for

speaking their native tongue at Shubenacadie.)

The next year, Sarah's father placed his two youngest daughters in Shubie, then went to work as a hunting guide in Bathurst, New Brunswick. Sarah took a trip to her birth place, Eel River Bar Reserve, to see her godmother, Phillip's sister Annie. Through Annie, Sarah found a job as a live-in housekeeper in the nearby town of Dalhousie. Sometimes Sarah walked to the reserve in the evening to visit with friends, including Janie Harquail who eventually introduced Sarah to her brother, Abe.

Abraham Harquail was born June 10, 1910, to Alexander and Marguerite Caron Harquail at Eel River Bar Reserve in New Brunswick. He had a younger brother, Jimmy, and a sister, Janie. Abe's parents were not basketmaking people. His father was the local barber and cultivated a subsistence garden for the family. His mother kept house and looked after the children. When Abe was only eight, his father died in a flu epidemic and Abe inherited the task of helping his family make a living. As Abe remembers it, he was too busy working to attend school: "I cut alder wood and cedar stump and sold the wood by handsleigh for twenty-five cents a load. I worked day and night sometimes. I was only about nine or ten years old."

At age twelve, Abe began helping an old basketmaker named Martin Pictou. "I cut ash for him, held the wood while he pounded it, and cleaned up for him—lugged out his shavings and burned them on the beach. Each week he used to give me a quarter or fifty cents or whatever he could spare."

At age thirteen, Abe went with Pictou's son Jim and several other fellows to pick potatoes in Maine. It was the **28** beginning of his life as a migratory seasonal laborer, echo-ing an age-old Micmac tradition. In the coming years he would alternately pick potatoes, work in potato houses, cut pulp, work on river drives, rake blueberries, pick fiddle-heads, make baskets, and trap fur-bearing animals.

When Abe was about fifteen, his mother married Billy Narvey, a Micmac who held the position of provincial con-stable on the reserve and who lived and worked seasonally in Maine and various corners of Canada. "Starting when I was eighteen," says Abe, "I worked with Billy as a trapper. Every year for eight years we trapped beaver, fox, sable, mink, anything we could get a hold of. We'd go up to Little Southeast [New Brunswick]. Stayed there for a month or two, minding a trap line that was fifteen miles long. We sold furs to Sam Rinsler in Dalhousie."

Abe's first recollection of making baskets himself is back in 1935 when he was twenty-five years old. That year, his younger brother Jimmy was working for Isaac Clements, a Micmac basketmaker at Restigouche Reserve in Quebec. Abe went north to join them for a while and took up the craft.

Now and again, in between seasonal work journeys, Abe came back to Eel River Bar and stayed with his sister Janie and her husband Tom Caplin. During a 1942 visit, he met Sarah. The next year they married. Sarah was sixteen, Abe was thirty-three. In July 1943, Sarah gave birth to Vincent, the first of their three children, born about one year apart.

One month later, Sarah and Abe went to Maine by train to pick potatoes, taking their new baby with them. "That's when I got into baskets," says Sarah. "Abe's brother Jimmy

Abe checking the sharpness of his draw shave, a two-handled knife used to carve ash sticks into hoops and handles or to square them off before pounding them into splints.

29

was there and he had a lot of basket orders he couldn't fill [on his own], so he taught me how to make bottoms." After that, says Sarah, "Abe and I moved about . . . and took our children with us wherever we went. . . . June and July we'd be making potato baskets in Aroostook. Then in August we'd go to Washington County to pick blueberries. Come September, we'd be back up here for potato season. After that, if we could find a good rent in Maine, we'd stay through the winter months. If not, we'd go north to the reserve. . . . Springtime we'd dig clams in Dalhousie or else pick fiddleheads in Aroostook. In between it all, I'd work in people's homes for a dollar a day—cooking, cleaning, and just looking after things."

In l949, due to Abe's struggle with alcoholism, Sarah left him, and eventually they divorced. She married three more times—first a Norwegian sea captain who died in a ship explosion, then a fellow who abused her until she left him, and finally a man for whom she'd kept house. The last marriage, says Sarah, "was one of convenience"—he was alone with his kids and Sarah with hers. Within three years alcohol got the best of him, and once again, Sarah set out on her own. A few years later, this last spouse died. Meanwhile, Abe was doing seasonal work, lumberjacking, harvesting potatoes and blueberries, digging clams, doing bridge construction, and selling firewood "as always."

For several years Sarah alternately picked potatoes and blueberries, made baskets, and kept house for people. In l970, when she was living in Caribou, Abe walked back into her life. "I asked him if he'd go into the basket business with me and he said yup. We've been together ever since." And they've been making baskets ever since, except during

Abe hand-pounding a stick of brown ash, which causes the year rings of the wood to separate. Each layer is a splint.

30

Sarah weaving the bottom of a potato basket. This step is usually done atop a hard flat surface.

periods when one of them has had health problems.

Three years ago their son Alex came to live with them following a divorce and a serious operation. Sarah nursed him back to health and soon had him helping with the basketmaking. "Alex helps an awful lot getting wood. And he makes baskets start to finish just about as good as me. I wanted to leave the tradition with someone, and it looks like he's the one."

Today baskets are a sideline for Sarah and Abe. "I'm no longer making them to put bread on the table," she says. "I have enough other resources, like a VA pension from [my last husband]. But when I don't make baskets for a month, my god, I miss it. I've been doing it for forty-six years and it's become a habit. You might say it's in my blood. In fact, if they opened my veins, they'd probably find them full of ash shavings."

Abe says he's still a basketmaker "because I have no other way to make a living and besides, I like making baskets and going into the woods to cut ash, and being near Sarah."

Donald Sanipass grew up in a time and culture that required intelligent use of one's hands to get by. He was born October 26, 1928, in Shediac, New Brunswick, the first of David and Margarite Labobe Sanipass' three sons. "I was brought up during the Depression, and we had to be self-sufficient to survive," he says. "My mother made baskets and Dad made axes, beautiful pine tables, and chairs with popple frames and alder seats. He trapped muskrat and beaver and sold the skins, and we ate muskrat stew and beaver legs." Sometimes Don went along when his father took off with his two-dogsled team to sell or barter skins and crafts. As Don recalls, the dog team consisted of "a couple of big mutts named Malty and Bear." Also, although Don didn't make baskets as a child, he did go into the woods with his father and grandfather to get ash wood for the craft.

In l935 Don's mother died of pneumonia. "It was hard times and Dad couldn't look after us kids alone, so he sent us to Shubenacadie [a Catholic mission school in Nova Scotia for Indian children]." Don stayed at Shubie until he was fifteen, then went to St. John, New Brunswick, where his father had moved to work dry dock construction. Don took up work at the war plant, building parts of the Mosquito Bomber, until the war ended. That same year, at age seventeen, he won the New Brunswick lightweight boxing title. For the next three years, he worked from construction job to construction job in St. John. Then he left the city and "started going back and forth between New Brunswick and

Mary splitting a thick splint with a splint splitter designed by her son David.

It's no picnic being a basketmaker. It's not what you call a good risk thing. But we get by—we keep the wolf man off the door. (D.S.)

Donald and Mary Lafford Sanipass
Chapman, Maine

Maine" for work, as had his father and his father's father before him.

Often Don went to Gouldsboro, Maine, where his uncle, Joe Daniel Sanipass, lived. "Uncle Daniel was cutting pulp part of the year," says Don, "and in the spring he was harvesting trap poles—young spruce limbs that could be bent to make lobster traps; he got five cents for a twenty-stick bundle." One weekend in 1952, Don met Mary Lafford who was in Gouldsboro visiting her brothers Harold and Henry, who were also doing seasonal work there. "I was cooking at Big Chief Sporting Camps in Sullivan," says Mary, "less than ten miles from Gouldsboro."

Mary was born in Antigonish, Nova Scotia, in 1935 to Louis and Susie Gould Lafford. Her father was a carpenter and a handyman. Her mother, often sickly, sometimes made baskets, but the steady basketmaker in the family was Mary's paternal grandmother, who often took care of Mary and her four siblings. Her grandparents, aunts, uncles, and cousins all lived nearby, and sometimes the whole extended family went "ash hunting" together. Says Mary, "We'd bed out three to four days in the woods until [the adults] got enough basket wood to last a month. We kids fished and snared rabbits. . . . Then, back at home, we watched on the side as our parents made baskets." By the time she was eight, says Mary, "I knew baskets. . . . I hadn't made my own yet, but I knew the process, including selling. I saw my parents, grammy, aunts, and uncles carry baskets to the train station to go to St. John to sell them."

Like Don, Mary went to Shubenacadie Residential School. She arrived there at age eight in 1943—just after Don's departure. "Both my parents got sick, so we kids left home

Donald loading his homemade toboggan with "basket wood" (brown ash). Photo by Mary Sanipass.

34

to go to Shubie. First Harold and Henry, then me, and three or four years later Annie and John. We had twelve nuns running the school. We weren't allowed to talk Indian. If we did, we got put to bed early with a spanking." Mary stayed at the school till she turned sixteen, then got the job at Big Chief Sporting Camps, not far from Gouldsboro, where she met Don.

A couple of months after Mary and Don met, they both went north to Mapleton to pick potatoes for John Carter. "After that fall," says Don, "me and Mary wanted to get married, but her folks didn't like the idea of her marrying me when she was so young. So we sneaked away . . . and eloped." They stayed in Boston several months, gave birth to their first child, Marlene, then moved to Fairvale, near St. John, where Don took up construction work. "Mary and I made dyed cedar picnic baskets when we lived in Fairvale," says Don. "We used to take the train to St. John, taking a load of baskets to sell." And, adds Mary, "I made little candy baskets and small fruit baskets of cedar for Nancy Nevins, a Micmac in Fairvale who bought and sold baskets. Don got the wood. His first cedar stick had a thousand knots in it and couldn't be split!"

In the summer of 1954, says Don, "we started going blueberrying in Cherryfield. After that first year, we went back again and again. . . . From then on it was blueberries in August, potatoes in the fall, then maybe to Canada for construction work. But by the sixties we were staying in Maine during the winter and spring to work in potato houses, cut seed, or do lumberjacking."

Until 1969, Don and Mary cut wood seasonally in northern Aroostook—for "jobbers" who had pulp contracts with

Donald rough-cutting a stick of ash with his ax. Photo by Mary Sanipass.

35

paper companies and also for local farmers. "You could go find yourself a job in the woods easy," says Don. "A lot of farmers were pulpers, too. They needed firewood to keep the potato houses warm enough so the potatoes didn't freeze. They used lots of wood."

Although basketry was a part-time occupation for Don and Mary throughout their marriage, Mary says they "didn't really get into baskets till we settled in Chapman in l967." Their house in Chapman, where they still live, is a converted camp, a place where they often stayed for potato picking season. The baskets they made throughout the l960s were primarily sturdy ash potato baskets, which earned them one or two dollars apiece. "If we were hard up we got seventy-five cents," says Mary. "Isn't that awful?"

During the l970s Don and Mary gradually decreased their potato work—cutting seed, harvesting, packaging—and increased their basket work. By 1982, when the dollar value of baskets began to climb, they were full-time basket-makers, producing a wide variety of utility baskets as well as some fancy ones. Don collects and prepares the ash, Mary does the weaving, and they both hoop and handle the baskets. It's physically grueling work, and they're often at it fourteen hours a day, yet the financial rewards remain modest at best. Says Don, "It's no picnic being a basket-maker. It's not what you call a good risk thing. But we get by—we keep the wolf man off the door." They have taught all four of their children each step of the craft. Their daugh-ter Roldena now makes her living as a basketmaker. Their son David is also an accomplished basketmaker but is best known for crafting beautiful knives with hand-carved handles of wood or antler. Their niece, twenty-one-year-old

Mary nailing a hoop on a picnic basket made of dyed and natural splints.

36

Cheryl Lafford, who they raised as one of their own children, still lives with Don and Mary and helps out with preparing splints and doing finishing work on baskets.

Today Don and Mary are probably the best-known basketmakers in Aroostook County. They have lived in the area for nearly three decades, and Don has served several terms as president of the Aroostook Micmac Council. They have given many basketry demonstrations throughout the state, and stories about them have appeared in statewide, New England, and national publications. Also, in 1985 they were featured in the fifty-minute color documentary film *Our Lives in Our Hands*. The many buyers who seek their quality work include store owners and dealers throughout the state, the Micmac Basket Bank, and a good number of individuals who follow stories of Don and Mary to their doorstep.

Wilfred Sanipass, known as "Wolf," was born March 23, 1932, in Shediac, New Brunswick, the youngest of David and Margarite Labobe Sanipass' three sons. His deepest memories include recollections of his father carving ax handles and getting wood for his mother's colored cedar baskets. And he remembers his father taking off by dogsled to barter the crafts for pork, flour, molasses, and other groceries. "From the time I was a little guy," he says, "I saw making baskets and ax handles as a way of life."

When Wolf was three, his mother died of pneumonia. "I was taken to my grandparents [at Big Cove Reserve in New Brunswick], for I was too young to go with my two brothers to Shubie [Shubenacadie Residential School for Indians]. My father went to St. John, New Brunswick, found [construction] employment, settled down, and eventually married again." At Big Cove, Wolf watched his grandfather tend the family garden, fish for herring, and "make baskets, ax handles—all the same things my father made."

At age seven, after finishing his first year of school at Big Cove, Wolf went to live with his father and stepmother. "We owned a radio and received newspapers," Wolf recalls—"something unheard of in Big Cove. . . . There were all kinds of "interesting and educational experiences for a young Micmac boy fresh off the reserve." The toughest part of life in St. John for Wolf was getting used to speaking English all the time. He spent his first two years in the same grade at school "due to the fact that I spoke mostly Micmac." Wolf's father continued to make ax handles for

Wilfred felling a cedar tree.

I don't do tomahawks or bows and arrows. Don't like white people coming up and asking for stereotype Indian stuff. I was a lumberjack, so my crafts are related to that. (W.S.)

Wilfred Sanipass
Chapman, Maine

extra money, and every summer he took Wolf to Big Cove to stay with his grandparents.

In 1948, when Wolf was sixteen, he got permission from his father to quit school and found a job in St. John's biggest hotel. He earned sixty dollars a month plus all he could eat. "That was a fortune for me," he recalls, "enough so I could help my parents out." But Wolf didn't wash dishes for long. He left that job to take up construction work, followed by dock work, followed by a job servicing and shining new cars at Lawson Motors. "Mike Lawson was a fan of Jim Thorpe, the Indian athlete who had won every event in the Olympic Games and was also a famous football player," recalls Wolf. "I'm no Jim Thorpe, but I'm Indian and that was all that mattered with Mike Lawson. I moved up a little faster than the older employees and felt a little guilty about it."

In the summer of 1952, while his father was visiting family in Jackman, Maine, Wolf "decided to cut the apron strings and join the Canadian army. I joined the First Division which had made itself quite famous during the war. I was stationed at St. George in New Brunswick—'Camp Utopia,' we called it. We did our maneuvers out in blueberry fields." In 1954 Wolf was discharged for medical reasons and headed to Aroostook County to work in the woods with his older brother Donald. Four years later, their father had a heart attack and decided to retire and move to Big Cove with his wife. "After that," recalls Wolf, "Dad lived on his pension and often came to visit us in Maine."

About 1960 Wolf met Micmac Mary Marshall of Nova Scotia during the potato harvest in northern Aroostook. "She was a beautiful basketmaker," he says. Wolf hadn't made baskets before, but it was a slack year for work, so he

Wilfred carving a block of cedar with his crooked knife.

39

took up the craft with Mary, who eventually became his common-law wife. He continued to work in the woods seasonally, and with Mary he worked in potato houses and followed the harvests—blueberries in Cherryfield and potatoes in Presque Isle. Every time there was a slack, they made baskets. In the 1960s, he says, "we were getting seventy-five cents for a potato basket and you could buy a lot for that back then. With the grocer we'd trade baskets for groceries. Or if we needed nails or sandpaper, we'd trade at the hardware. Or we just peddled the baskets farmer to farmer. You could sell them year-round back then; farmers never had enough baskets."

After Mary died in 1978, Wolf gave up making baskets for sale and "got serious" about wood carving, which he'd played with for some five years. He had no teacher, other than many memories of his father carving ax handles through the years. But he was very familiar with wood and knives from his years of lumberjacking and basketry. "When you make baskets, you're always carving," he says. "You use a draw shave or crooked knife to make handles and hoops or runners for pack baskets. And you carve with an ax to shape the ash out before pounding it." Wolf was always very involved with the knives he used in basketry, so much so that he made them himself. "If you need a tool, you make it. You just take a pattern from your parents, copy it, and then adjust it a bit to fit your style. . . . The first knife I made was an ax, then a crooked knife, then a draw knife."

Gradually, carving eclipsed Wolf's seasonal jobs. He stopped picking potatoes in 1968, quit lumberjacking in 1977, gave up basketry in 1978, stopped all potato house work in 1982, and raked his last blueberries in 1984. "Since 1984,

Wilfred sitting atop his shaving horse, carving.

40

carving has been a steady self-employed profession for me," he says.

In l986 Wolf married Lorette Ray, whom he met at a small business workshop in Bangor. Lorette is keenly interested in Native American culture and also does traditional crafts, including bone and bead jewelry. "She's more Indian than I am!" laughs Wolf. "Before I met her, she was adopted by the Crow Indians and given the name 'Spirit Woman.'"

Today Wolf and Lorette live in a small camp alongside his brother Donald's place. In addition to making real tools which he sells to basketmakers, Wolf carves all-wood models of early lumberjack tools. "I liked the lumberjack scene I was involved in," he says, "and like to bring the tools from those days back—the tools this country was carved with." With this in mind, Wolf makes miniature and life-sized wood replicas of the broad ax and double bidder, the bucksaw and pulp hook, the "hoe" which was used for hewing beams, and the twitch chain with hook and binder. "I also carve scissors, hammers, and miniatures of all basket tools," he says. "I carve anything that fancies my eye, even nuts and bolts."

Wolf does all of his carving with a crooked knife and always works in cedar, a soft, easy-to-handle wood. "I don't use just any ordinary cedar," he says. "I go cruisin' the woods, find a cedar swamp where beavers have dropped the trees or a swail where cedar's been dead for years and sat in the sun so long that it's almost white. It's a lot prettier than the green kind." Then, says Wolf, he turns to the wood for guidance. "It's not you that handles the wood; it's the wood that leads you—its grain, color, texture."

Although Wolf says he would like to leave the wood natural, he's found that when "you buff cedar down so smooth, it has to be protected or it will soil and even a fingernail will leave an imprint." So he stains each finished piece and then adds two coats of polyurethane, "sanding in between each one."

Wolf sells his work through the Aroostook Micmac Council, at fairs around the state, and to individuals who follow his reputation and arrive at his camp to buy one of his pieces. He says that one of the things he likes about his work is watching people pick up a piece. "They brace themselves, expecting it to be heavy, and then, Wow! It's light. They always have such a surprised look on their faces."

On June 23, 1931, Harold was born to Louis and Susie Gould Lafford at Afton Reserve, Nova Scotia, the first of five children. "There were some more kids," says Harold, "but they died real young." Louis was a carpenter, basketmaker, and handyman, and moved around a lot looking for work opportunities in Maine and the Maritimes. Susie made baskets and occasionally did factory work, but she was often sickly and frequently went to stay with her parents in Eskasoni, Nova Scotia. Frequently, Louis's parents, Isabelle and William Lafford took care of Harold and his siblings.

As far back as Harold can remember, whether with his parents or grandparents, the family moved often to find work. Mostly they lived in small hamlets surrounding St. John, New Brunswick. "We moved from Fairvale to Hampton to Broomfield, then back," he recalls, "and we always lived near a woods where we could get ax handle and basket wood [white ash and cedar]." In those days, says Harold, his family used cedar rather than brown ash for baskets. It was easier to find in that region and it took less energy to prepare than basket ash. Often the whole extended family went into the woods for several days at a time to gather the raw materials they needed for their crafts.

Sometimes the Laffords set up camp on a farmer's land— such as in Hampton, where Harold's father did odd jobs for the farmer and worked at a nearby mill and where his grandparents made baskets and other wood products. They sold their utility baskets to farmers or the local grocer. When living in Fairvale, they sometimes cut through the

Harold weaving a picnic basket.

All I'm educated to do is work in the woods and make baskets. When you ain't got nothing to do, you got to do something. So I do this. I'm my own boss. Got nobody to tell me nothing. Nobody hollering at me. And nobody paying me—unless I make a basket. (H.L.)

Harold Lafford
Chapman, Maine

woods to the little town of Rossi where they could sell all kinds of baskets to a Micmac named Nancy Nevins who made her living buying and selling Indian crafts. In most of the hamlets they lived in they could flag down the train and ride to St. John where they could sell a variety of baskets at the big open market. Harold recalls that "there were quite a few Indians there selling whatever they could make—cedar shopping baskets, sewing baskets, knitting baskets, fruit baskets, ax handles." Sometimes the train station was their overnight refuge.

Harold's education opportunities were slim. As the oldest child, he was often charged with caring for his siblings. His sister Mary recalls that "it was mostly Harold who took care of us. When my parents went to work at Crosby's Molasses Factory in St. John, Harold stayed home with us and got our breakfast for us. I guess school just wasn't that important to a lot of people in those days."

When Harold did go to school, it was in Rossi, about two miles from Fairvale. "Sometimes I walked through the woods to get there and sometimes I took the bus," he recalls. But with so much moving about and so many things to tend to at home, progress at school was slow. By age twelve, Harold was still in the second grade. That year, says Harold, "the Indian agent showed up at our place and said we kids would have to go to Shubie [Shubenacadie Residential School in Nova Scotia]." A week later, the agent took Harold by train. "I didn't know where I was going," says Harold, "but I was going." The other children came later.

"Shubie was pretty good. We'd go to school and take turns going to the dairy barn early in the morning to milk the cows. We had nuns for teachers. I got tired of staying there, but they treated us nice. I stayed straight through for three years. When I came out, my parents were in Fairvale and I went back there. I got wood for them and worked out for other people, mowing lawns, cutting firewood, and running errands. Then I went to Ontario to work the river drive. There were Iroquois Indians working there too. We worked sixty miles back in the woods, breaking up jams. It took six sticks of dynamite to undo a big jam. One time I didn't know they were gonna blow, and I got knocked down and soaking wet. Then I worked on a railroad crew making new tracks." After little more than a month in Ontario, Harold returned to Fairvale, then moved on to Ashville, Maine.

In Ashville, Harold stayed with his aunt and uncle, Lizzie and Noel Phillips, who made their living cutting pulpwood in the fall and spring, raking berries and digging clams in the summer, doing road maintenance in the winter, and making baskets to sell roadside in between time. They lived near the water in a converted garage with a one-room annex which they called "the lodging camp." Harold took up cutting pulp with his relatives. "[The whole family] went in the woods together," he remembers, "grandfather, kids, and all."

In 1949, at age eighteen, Harold went to blueberry country in Cherryfield for the first time and "worked for a guy named Bud Randall, cutting wood, marking off the fields, raking and hauling blueberries." After two years he went to Boston and worked at the Parker House Hotel running stock from the liquor room to the bar.

City life was by no means Harold's final destination. He soon returned to Maine. "I went up to Gouldsboro and met up with [my brother-in-law] Donald [Sanipass]. We did odd jobs, blueberry work, cutting pulp. Around 1952 we started

43

going up to Aroostook County after blueberry season to pick potatoes. We'd just go to a farmer and ask if he needed pickers. He'd say he could handle a few, so we'd have ourselves a little job. The farmers had camps or picker's houses for us to stay in."

It was not until l960 that Harold started making baskets, spurred on by his sister Mary who was making potato baskets for farmers. He says he had seen his father and grandfather make baskets so often that he just knew what to do. "It took a little while before I got on to good baskets. But once I learned the potato basket, I started learning everything, pack baskets, you name it."

The next year Harold met a Micmac named Susie Scully from Prince Edward Island. "We met pickin' berries and stayed together right steady for almost thirty years." That same year he began working for Jasper Wyman in Cherryfield. "I did everything with Wyman's blueberry lands—driving a tractor and dusting the fields around May, marking off the fields for pickers, hauling berries, then mowing down the fields at the end of the season. I worked until the frost came, usually around the end of September. Worked for Wyman fifteen years." While he tended the fields, Susie kept house. When Harold had time to find wood for her, she made baskets, and each August she raked berries.

During the winters of his Wyman years, Harold worked in the woods in Cherryfield for Henry Rinski, a foreman for Pejepscot Paper Company. "The only thing I didn't like was driving the skidder," he says. "You've always got to hurry. One time a stick almost drove through my stomach, and another time a brake let go and a skidder almost ran over me." While working in the woods, Harold and Susie lived in

Harold sectioning off a prime lower cut of brown ash—the upper reaches of the trunk are too brittle for baskets.

a small camp supplied by Rinski. As usual, Susie cooked, kept house, and made baskets.

When Harold grew weary of lumberjacking, he and Susie "took a rest up in Aroostook and made baskets. I got the wood, she did the weaving, and I hooped and handled. Susie could make everything—small little teeny baskets right up to the big ones. But mostly we made potato baskets—just enough baskets to live on."

In 1980, Susie and Harold moved into a one-room camp next door to his sister Mary's place in Chapman. Harold has lived in Aroostook year-round since then, except for his annual summer trip to rake blueberries in Cherryfield. In 1983 Susie was nearly sixty. Homesick and in poor health, she returned to the reserve she'd grown up on at Lennox Island, Prince Edward Island. There she had the health support system she needed and a chance to reunite with her children from a much earlier marriage. Harold has not seen her since, but they talk often on the phone.

Today Harold lives alone and, other than raking blueberries, survives on his baskets. "I've been a serious basketmaker for twenty-five years now," he says. "All my baskets are nice and tight. I keep steady on each basket to make it good. Take my time and see if I can get it just right." By the time Harold Lafford finishes a basket, he has spent enough time with it to make it a friend. Buyers, drawn by the tight weave and carefully shaped lines of Harold's baskets come right to his doorstep. "I don't have to go anywhere. They come to me," he says. But they don't come often enough or stay long enough to keep him company. He relies on his baskets for that. "Baskets are good company," he says, "the only company I've got nowadays."

Harold on snowshoes, loading his homemade toboggan with basket ash. (Note: Toboggan is hooked to a snowmobile.)

45

On January 26, l932, Mary Jane Zumbrunnen was born to Billy and Angelique Condo Jerome at Maria Reserve on Chaleur Bay in the Province of Quebec. She is the fourth of five children born between 1926 and l943.

Mary Jane, known as Jane, says her early childhood memories include watching her mother weaving baskets and her father making snowshoes and preparing ash splints. Her father also worked as a hunting and fishing guide in the Maritime provinces and Maine. Like many other Micmac families, the Jeromes moved back and forth between Maine and Canada, following work opportunities.

When Jane was ten years old, her mother died. "We were in Presque Isle picking potatoes and they found her dead in the bed," she recalls. "I don't know what she died of." Jane's father returned to Maria Reserve and, with the help of family members and his oldest daughter, Annie Mae, managed to keep his three youngest children together. His oldest son, Louie, had already married and lived next door.

Two years after her mother's death, Jane's father also died. "He drowned while guiding rich people," says Jane. By this time, Annie Mae was living permanently in Maine. Jane and her little sister Bernadette moved in with their big brother Louie and his wife. Her brother Raymond moved in with their aunt and uncle, John and Mary Condo, who had a place at Maria.

From this point, Jane's Aunt Mary and Uncle John played a significant role in Jane's life. Mary not only made baskets herself but bought and sold the work of other Micmac basketmakers. "She had a grocery store on the reserve," says

Jane signing one of her fancy baskets. She's wearing one of the many novelty items she weaves—an ash splint hat.

I don't like to sit around. So I like baskets— gives me something to do. And there's money in basketmaking; if you get stuck, you know where to go. (J.Z.)

Jane Jerome Zumbrunnen
Caribou, Maine

Jane, "and used to send basket orders out from there . . . [or sell them to] tourists who came through in buses."

Jane remembers helping her aunt with baskets. "Aunt Mary made fancy baskets and I wrapped the tops and made little rings on the lids. Her husband prepared all the wood and my brother Raymond helped pound the ash and everything." Jane also remembers selling baskets roadside for her aunt, along with her cousin. It was while waiting for customers to happen along that Jane first made an entire basket on her own. "I sat down at that little shack by the road and took a splint and said to myself, 'Let me try to make one little basket myself.' It was just a plain little candy basket without curlicues, not perfect, but I sold it for twenty cents. After that, I kept trying and got better. My aunt was glad."

When she was sixteen, Jane went back to Maine. "I stayed with my sister Annie Mae and got a job at the Elite Restaurant in Caribou, cooking and doing dishes." Over the next few years she got by on restaurant work and seasonal potato work.

In 1956, when Jane was twenty-four, she married a Micmac fellow named Arnold Martin in Caribou, and soon thereafter the young couple moved up to Maria Reserve. "My husband worked as an ash crew member with my Uncle John, and I made baskets—fancy baskets, wastepaper baskets, and little sweethay brooms. I used to buy a lot of stuff from my basket money—furniture, my stove, my washer."

Jane and Arnold had eight children and stayed together for twenty years. In 1976 the couple divorced and Jane moved back to Caribou. A year or so later, she met Charles Zumbrunnen, stationed at Loring Air force base. They married, and she spent most of her time keeping house for him.

In her spare moments, she knit stockings, slippers, and afghans and sold them to local customers. Periodically she took her handmade slippers up to Maria and sold them through the reserve's craft cooperative.

"I never made baskets in Maine until about five years ago," says Jane. "It was the [Micmac Council] Basket Bank that made me start thinking of baskets again." Reminded of her "old times of selling baskets," she decided to take up the craft again. Her brother Raymond was in the area and she asked him to get and prepare an ash log for her. "I didn't have [basket] tools, so I just used scissors." After making several fancy baskets, she brought them to the Basket Bank and sold them.

Jane became so involved with basketry that in 1986 the Micmac Council hired her to run its small basket shop, teach basketry workshops, and produce specialty baskets to help fill customer orders. She has continued with that job ever since.

Today Jane spends even her spare time at home making baskets, and her fancy splint baskets are recognized as among the finest produced in Maine. She's the last basketmaker in her family, and she regrets that. "I taught my eight children baskets when they were little," she says. "But they don't want to do it, and you can't tell them what to do." But this year she received a Maine Art Commission grant as a master basketmaker to provide basketry training for a Micmac apprentice. So she has an opportunity to pass the craft on after all. She believes the craft is worthwhile not only for tradition's sake but "because there's money in it." Once you know basketry, she says, "if you get stuck [financially], you know where to go."

Ruby Tenas Schillinger was born October 12, 1933, at Eel Ground Reserve near New Castle, New Brunswick, to Peter and Mary Swasson Tenas. "They had fourteen kids," says Ruby, "but a lot of my brothers and sisters died before I was even born." Ruby doesn't remember seeing her father working when she was young, but she does recall her mother and grandmother working hard around the house. "Mom and Grandma kept a garden and did canning every year." They also made baskets. "When I first saw anyone making baskets," says Ruby, "it was my grandmother, my father's mother. She lived with us. She didn't make baskets all the time—just when we ran out of tobacco or something she'd make some. It was the only thing she knew how to do, other than just be a housewife. Probably my father got wood for her." Ruby says her mother and grandmother made a variety of baskets, including potato baskets. "They left the handles off and stacked the baskets inside each other and took them to the train. Must have been shipping them someplace, maybe Maine."

Ruby had almost no opportunity for education. "My schoolin' ended before I got started," she says. "We had a white teacher in a one-room schoolhouse on the reserve, but I got kicked out when I was a real little girl. They said I couldn't learn because I couldn't speak English."

Not long after being dismissed from school, Ruby left Eel Ground with her mother and her older sister Theresa. "Mom and Dad weren't getting along good and Dad went in the army, so Mother, Theresa, and me went to Maine."

Ruby sitting on her shaving horse, using a draw shave knife to square off a stick of ash.

Nobody really taught me baskets. You weren't supposed to bother [adults] when they were working. . . . I just watched my mother . . . picked up leftover wood she threw away and tried to make some little basket exactly like her. Mine looked real funny. (R.S.)

Ruby Tenas Schillinger
Smyrna Mills, Maine

Theresa was about a year older than me and I think we were the only children left." Throughout the next decade, Mary and her two daughters moved all about Maine looking for seasonal work. "We went to Bangor, Bar Harbor, Mars Hill, Presque Isle, Houlton. . . ." says Ruby. "We all picked potatoes in the fall . . . and Mom used to cut pulp . . . Rest of the time we stayed in some old farmhouse and made baskets. . . . We [kids] helped her with anything she had to do. When she went in the woods, so did we. We helped with the work horse or with the buck saw. I was about ten when I first went with her in the woods."

Ruby says it was shortly after they moved to Maine that her mother "taught" her to make baskets. Actually, she says, "nobody really taught me. . . . You weren't supposed to bother [adults] when they were working. . . . I just watched my mother . . . picked up leftover wood she threw away and tried to make some little basket exactly like her. Mine looked real funny. It was way after I was married that I made my own first basket to sell."

Ruby met her husband, Eldon Schillinger, a white man from Linneus, at a lumber camp near Houlton. "My mother was cooking for a bunch of lumberjacks in a camp and Eldon was one of them. I helped out in the kitchen, doing dishes, peeling potatoes. I was quite young when [Eldon and I] met. He's ten years older than me." Several years later, she ran into Eldon "right there in the street in Houlton," says Ruby. "I went with him for nine months, then married him. I was eighteen."

Ruby and Eldon moved around for work. "Eldon could do anything," she says, "construction, lumberjacking, mechanics, potato work." Frequently they lived with

Ruby using an ax and maul to splint a brown ash log into "sticks."

49

Ruby pounding a stick of ash with her homemade electric pounder. This causes the year rings of the wood to separate. Each layer is a splint.

50

Ruby splitting an overly-thick splint with her teeth and hands.

Ruby using her crooked knife to scrape a splint smooth.

51

Eldon's brother who had a small potato farm in Limerick. They helped him bring in his crop and provided him with potato baskets. "Once I learned that making baskets meant I could make money, stay home, take care of the kids and do cooking, I did it every day," says Ruby. "I made anything—potato baskets, laundry, hamper, pack, sewing, comb. . . . You name it, I made it. Potato baskets was always in greatest demand. I sold mostly to farmers." Eldon usually helped out. "He got pretty good at baskets for a white man, getting my wood, helping with hoops and handles."

Ruby also wove ash splint chair seats. "People would bring them over to me," she says. "But now I'm starting to forget how to do that because people haven't brought them by for a long time."

In 1964 Ruby and Eldon settled in Smyrna Mills where they continued to do potato work and make baskets, and Eldon found long-term work as an auto mechanic for two different garages. The couple remains in Smyrna today, along with some of their children. "Our kids and grandchildren come and go regularly," says Ruby. "At the moment, it's me and Eldon and [my daughter] Carla and her little girl living here. [And my sons] Jimmy and Michael also. Mike's twenty-one and Jimmy's seventeen."

Ruby continues to make baskets, and although Eldon retired recently, he still helps her by getting wood. "Eldon goes into the woods, spots a good tree, and cuts it for me," says Ruby, "but he makes Mike or Jimmy carry it out because he can't [do much physical] work now." Ruby prepares all her own wood—splitting, pounding, and scraping. Although this task is eased a bit by the electric ash pounder Eldon got in Island Falls over twenty years ago, Ruby has

slowed down her production during the last year because of her own health problems. "I always thought I was tough as a horse, but last year I had a heart attack so haven't been able to work as hard. But when we need something, I [still] make baskets."

Ruby has taught some of her children to make baskets, and her daughter Carla works at the craft now and then. Ruby has taught other people as well. "I went over to the Head Start school where my grandchildren go and showed the kids how to do it. My grandkids said, 'We see Grammy do that all the time so we don't want to do it.' But those other little kids, they learned so fast." Ruby has also given basketry demonstrations at the Abbe Museum in Bar Harbor. But one of her favorite demonstration stories is the one about a man who paid her just to watch her work. "A guy came here from Massachusetts or someplace and wanted to watch me prepare the wood. I did it all and it took some time and when I was finished he gave me twenty dollars!"

Such bonuses are rare, Ruby admits, which is one reason basketry has always been only a portion of her livelihood. As Ruby puts it, "Lots of times there are things I need that I can't afford—so I make a basket so I can buy it. Just like [my grandmother]: when you need something, make a basket."

On March 23, 1934, Joe Silliboy was born in St. John, New Brunswick, to Mary Phillips Silliboy. Before Joe's birth, his father, Steven Silliboy, died in an accident when jumping a train on one of his seasonal migratory labor routes near Vanceboro in Washington County, Maine. When Joe was six, his mother and her three little boys moved to Gouldsboro, Maine, where they lived in a modest camp with a fabulous view of Frenchman Bay. "That's when I first started learning baskets," says Joe. "My family always made baskets when we lived there."

Mary's mother, Annie Battiste Phillips, also lived in Gouldsboro for a while, as did Mary's brother Noel and his family. They often worked collectively on baskets. Says Joe, "The men and the boys got wood for the women's fancy baskets. Back then we used to make baskets out of cedar and maple which you can strip by hand without pounding. . . . I made little [baskets] four to five inches across. Mom made lots of sewing baskets. She dyed the splints with Diamond dye and also made dye out of crepe paper, especially yellow, blue, and green. Mom also used sweetgrass." Sometimes Joe's family sold their baskets roadside to tourists visiting the coast. Other times, says Joe, "my mother would make a lot and then take them to Ellsworth to sell. . . . She could make the prettiest baskets you ever saw; I wish I had one of them today. I tried to buy some of her baskets back from people in Houlton, but they wouldn't part with them."

In addition to helping the adults make baskets, Joe and his siblings used to dig clams and worms to help the family

Joe weaving the sides of a potato basket—a task often done on one's lap.

When I was a boy and we lived by the coast, we sold baskets along the highway. We'd hang 'em out along the road. Tourists came and we couldn't make enough baskets to satisfy them. (J.S.)

Joseph Patrick Silliboy
Littleton, Maine

make a living. "You could make a pretty good living out of the ocean," he says. "We had a rowboat and we fished for smaller fish that you could catch with a line in shallow water—mackerel and flounder. Sold 'em for twenty-eight cents a pound. . . . We went to school, but when the tide was down we'd be out clamming right after school or in the night."

Like his older brothers, Joe learned about working in the woods from his Uncle Noel, as well as from his mother. By the time he was eleven, Joe says, "I used to walk seven miles into the woods on my own and cut two to three cords of pulpwood with a bucksaw before coming out. I worked for a man named Charlie Small." By this time, Joe had quit school altogether, as had his older brothers. "We kids figured we had to work to help out. Mother worked hard doing every kind of work you can imagine. She was an awful nice woman. She and my grandmother went all out for us kids."

Around 1946, Mary and her kids moved up to Aroostook for the potato harvest. By that time Mary had given birth to ten children. Three had died as infants and one had been given up for adoption because Mary was ill during his infancy and unable to care for him. In 1947, she had her last child, Richard. Her oldest child, Matthew, was then seventeen.

In 1951, after living several places in southern Aroostook, Mary moved with her six sons and one daughter to a fourteen-by-twenty-four-foot camp built by potato farmer Clarence Shaw in Littleton. Here she stayed for fourteen years, her children working as farm hands for Shaw, she making potato baskets for him and a variety of other baskets

Joe hand-pounding a stick of ash with the blunt edge of his ax. This causes the year rings of the wood to separate, yielding splints.

which she sold door to door.

Joe, like his siblings, came and went seasonally from the Littleton camp, following work opportunities. He worked in the woods and lumber mills, did road construction, raked blueberries for two weeks each summer, picked potatoes three weeks in the fall, cut potato seed for three weeks in the spring, and sometimes took a winter job with McKeay Construction—spending one hundred hours a week chipping ice off the box cars of Bangor and Aroostook Railway. Whenever there was no other work available, he made baskets.

In 1955 Joe married Roberta Flewelling, a Maliseet, and continued working as a seasonal laborer. Together they had eight children, the first in 1956, the last in 1971. The children have chosen work very different from that of their father—one manages the local McDonalds, another is a carpenter, another an auto repairman. The youngest, Mary Lou, attends the University of Maine in Machias.

In 1981 Joe decided to become a full-time basketmaker, interrupting the trade only to rake blueberries in August, pick potatoes in September, and cut potato seed in April. He made the choice for health reasons but also because the increased value of handmade wood splint baskets has made the craft a viable, if modest, livelihood. "Now I can sell as many baskets as I make. If I had a million I could sell them," says Joe. Sometimes he sells through his brother Richard Silliboy's new business, Three Feathers. But Joe has long-term clients he's beholden to. "I've had dealers coming to me for ten years, mostly antique dealers and shop owners,"

he says. "I sell mostly medium potato baskets with nailed hoop and get about twelve dollars apiece. I do all my pounding by hand and still get the wood myself—pay Great Northern fifteen dollars a cord to cut it on their land."

Richard Silliboy came at the end of the line of Mary Phillips Silliboy's eleven children. He was born March 3, 1947, in Gouldsboro, Maine, where his mother and older brothers worked seasonally clamming, making baskets, raking blueberries, and cutting pulp and firewood. "Mom was a tough go-getter," says Richard. "She worked and fought like a man, and some of my brothers treated her like one."

When Richard was three and his oldest brother was twenty, Mary moved her brood to a fourteen-by-twenty-four-foot camp built by Clarence Shaw, a potato farmer in Littleton. The humble abode was part of Shaw's payment for work supplied by the Silliboy family. "Mother made potato baskets for him, and whichever boys were around brought in potatoes and hay and did other work as needed."

Not long after the move, Mary's boys added another room to the camp—a bedroom with a cot and two bunk beds where they slept. Mary slept in the front room, as did Richard until he was older. "Mother sat on her bed making baskets," he recalls. "There were splints everywhere, including on my bed. In fact, each night when I crawled under the covers, I also crawled under the splints."

The itinerant Silliboy youths came and went with the change of seasons—as did other Micmac migrants who sometimes stayed at Mary's place. Mary decided what baskets to make and what material to use based on who was on hand to help her. Says Richard, "When the boys were around and she had a lot of help getting and preparing ash, she'd focus on potato baskets. But when working on her

Richard positioning the handle on a potato basket.

Because I was the youngest of eleven kids, I was always the one elected to go with Mother door to door selling baskets. She'd fill my arms with sewing, pie, and picnic baskets and we'd hit the higher class side of town. (R.S.)

Richard Silliboy
Littleton, Maine

own, it was easier to make fancy baskets with cedar which could be stripped by hand without pounding. She made a lot of pie and candy baskets out of cedar."

During these years, Richard's involvement in the basketry trade consisted of watching, holding the light when his brothers pounded ash at night, and traipsing door-to-door with his mother to sell the goods. Unlike his big brothers who'd left school after third or fourth grade to take paid jobs, Richard was able to complete junior high before quitting to find work.

He did a variety of jobs typical among Micmacs—harvesting potatoes, working in potato houses, raking berries, cutting pulp, doing millwork. He also worked as a shipping agent and a machine operator. But he didn't make baskets. "Although I came from a basketmaking family, I wasn't interested in it because of the terrible value of baskets in the County. I saw my mother work so hard and get so little out of it. That discouraged me. But I was always interested in baskets. At different times I'd go out and get wood and experiment with cedar and ash, making baskets but never to sell."

In 1966 Richard married Linda Lou Lorom. They have two sons and two daughters, who range in age from fourteen to twenty-three. In 1986, Richard passed the high school equivalency test and gained employment as manager of the Aroostook Micmac Council Basket Bank, a marketing and distribution center for Micmac basketmakers. This job gave him the opportunity to do sales outside of Aroostook County. At crowd-drawing events such as the annual Maine Festival and the Common Ground Fair, says Richard, "I saw how popular splint baskets had become and discovered

Richard securing a hoop on a potato basket by wrapping it with a splint.

57

there was a great market for them beyond the farmers who were used to paying low prices." Bit by bit, he became interested in making baskets himself. "At the fairs, people would stop to talk about baskets, asking if I'd made them. When I said I was just buying and selling them, it turned people away—and it made me feel like a non-Indian sales- man. So I decided to do something about it."

Certainly Richard knew what to do. He had prepared wood for some of the fancy basketmakers who sold through the Basket Bank. He had refurbished baskets that weren't quite up to the Bank's standard before offering them for sale. He knew which baskets were in greatest demand. Plus, his mind was packed with childhood recollections of this craft. "I took up making medium wrapped-hoop potato baskets because I knew that was the big seller. Of course my baskets were floppy at first, but I got it down with time."

Richard became the fourth of Mary Silliboy's sons to rely on basketry for a livelihood. Two, Matthew and John, are now deceased. The third, Joe, still carries on the tradition. Today Richard has his own basket business in Houlton, Three Feathers, through which he markets his work as well as that of Joe and other Native Americans in the region.

Richard in front of his new shop, Three Feathers, where he sells his baskets along with the works of other Wabanaki craftspeople.

58

Eldon Hanning learned basketry from his mother, Elizabeth Knockwood Hanning. As a young child, Elizabeth was placed in the St. Vincent Orphanage in Charlottetown, Prince Edward Island, in 1916. Her father had been killed in World War I, and her mother was not able to support her alone. At age fourteen, Elizabeth finally left the orphanage to be with her mother on Lennox Island, P. E. I. There, she recalls, "I started making baskets with my mother. She had made them all her life and told me her mother and grand-mother had made them too. I never saved one of my mother's baskets—guess I traveled too much to carry one around."

Like most Micmacs of her generation, Elizabeth did travel a lot. After an unsuccessful marriage to Micmac Jacob Labobe in Nova Scotia, she went to Houlton, Maine, in the mid–1930s to pick potatoes. There she met Ben Hanning, a Maliseet who had grown up in the area. "I stayed there, married Ben, and taught him to get wood and make baskets," says Elizabeth. "He was good at it and we lived on baskets, along with picking potatoes in the fall and raking berries in Cherryfield in the summer. We usually traded our baskets for food at the grocers." In Houlton, on August 5, 1951, Elizabeth gave birth to Eldon, the youngest of Ben's and her four children.

Shortly thereafter the Hanning family moved down to Millbridge, near Cherryfield. "My father worked in the woods, and in the summer he and my mother picked berries and dug clams," says Eldon. "In the fall, we all came

As far as I know, I'm the only Micmac in Maine making giant potato baskets—four feet across, big enough to sit in. My son makes inch-and-a-half miniature potato baskets that he sells for $1.50 apiece. So it seems we make the littlest and biggest baskets in the County. (E.H.)

Eldon pounding a stick of ash with his electric pounder, causing the year rings of the wood to separate and yield splints.

Eldon Hanning
Limestone, Maine

up to Houlton to work the potato harvest. My father taught me that wherever we went there was work of some kind."

In 1959 they all moved back to Aroostook County and over the next few years lived in several towns—Ft. Fairfield, Limestone, Presque Isle, Mapleton, Easton, Washburn. Ben worked in potato houses and in the woods and made baskets with Elizabeth. Says Eldon, "As a kid I was always around baskets, picking them up, playing with them, seeing my parents make them. Far back as I can remember, they went into the woods for ash. All we had was a regular sedan. They'd take out the back seat, open up the trunk, and slide in six-foot logs of ash. Used to load it right up, leaving enough room for my sister Roberta and me to crawl up on top of the pile. There we'd lie between the wood and the roof top."

In 1964 the family moved back to Houlton. Eldon was in and out of school, more interested in earning a little cash than sitting behind a school desk. "A farmer named Harry Bass used to come get me out of school to work and I'd jump at the chance. . . . He'd tell me to pick enough guys for a job, and I'd choose my cousins and off we'd go to make $1.65 an hour—hauling potato seed from a train car onto a truck to take to his farm. We were fast, could unload two cars a day." At age sixteen, Eldon quit school for good and went to work cutting pulp and cedar in the woods.

Come 1971, Eldon joined the U.S. Army and spent the next ten years moving about from station to station—Korea, Texas, Kentucky, Panama, Colorado. While in Korea, he passed his high school equivalency test, married a Korean woman, and had a son, Frank. Frank was born in 1973, the same year Eldon's father died of cancer.

Eldon weaving a large potato basket.

60

Eldon measuring a handle for a small potato basket.

When Eldon quit the service in 1981, he and his wife separated, and their son went with her. Eldon returned to Maine and lived in Van Buren and Houlton before settling in Presque Isle. He did various odd jobs, including work at Al Irving's potato house.

In Presque Isle, Eldon visited the Micmac Council's Basket Bank—a marketing and distribution center for Micmac basketmakers. "I hadn't seen or touched ash in ten years," he says, "but what I saw at the Basket Bank encouraged me. I came up with a plan to do potato house work in the day and make baskets at night. I had my mother move up from Oakfield to show me what I'd forgotten or didn't know about making baskets. My first few were rickety, but I got better."

Today Eldon lives in Limestone and makes baskets full time. "I go through about one hundred logs a year and each makes about twenty baskets—so I make about two thousand baskets a year." His son, Frank, who came to live with him in 1984, helps out. "Frank used to pound ash by hand for me," says Eldon, "but now I have an electric ash pounder. I take care of splitting the logs, squaring off the sticks, and feeding them into the pounder. Then Frank splits [any overly-thick] splints by hand, and shaves them smooth." In addition to making baskets, Eldon sells ash logs and prepared splints as well as handmade gauges, crooked knives, and draw shaves. His mother, Elizabeth, continues to live with Eldon. Pleased that one of her children is carrying on this tradition, she sometimes weaves for him. "I still like working on baskets," she says. "If I were a million years old, I'd still do it. Baskets are my life."

David Sanipass, one of the most versatile Micmac craftsmen in Aroostook, is the third of Donald and Mary Sanipass' four children—and their only son. He was born in Ellsworth, Maine, November 11, 1958, a year when his parents remained in Washington County to cut pulpwood after working the blueberry harvest.

David grew up in Aroostook County, surrounded by wood and metal crafts. His parents and his uncles Harold and Henry Lafford made baskets and basketry tools; his uncle Wilfred Sanipass made baskets, woodcarvings, and a great variety of woodworking and lumberjack tools; and his grandfather, David Sanipass, made "just about everything."

"I think one of my earliest memories of baskets is playing in the splints and then my grampa showing me how to take scraps and roll 'em up and tie 'em into a ball to play with. Another early basket memory is going into the woods to help my father get ash when I was about eleven. I remember him talking about the grains of the trees and telling me that each splint represented one year ring in the tree. When we left the woods, he'd carry a log on his back and I'd drag one."

David says he learned basketry the same way his father did "by watching. Dad told me, 'Just watch, and when you feel ready, do it.' Then I'd do it and he and Mom would look at the work and show me where I'd gone right and where I'd gone wrong. Mom always said, 'You have to make a basket wrong before you can learn to do it right.'"

Eventually David learned how to make every basket that his parents made. But, more than baskets caught his atten-

David at his outside work table.

When I was about seven years old, my mother didn't allow me to have a sharp knife. I got a butter knife, sharpened it with my dad's stone, and kept it under my mattress. I remember carving a bird, a plane, and a bear with that knife. (D.S.)

David Sanipass
Presque Isle, Maine

tion. He developed a keen interest in wood carving, born of "watching my grandfather sitting by a fire at night carving little owls and deer out of cedar." Although his mother didn't allow him to have a sharp knife when he was small, David recalls that when he was seven years old, "I got a butter knife, sharpened it with my dad's stone, and kept it under my mattress. I remember carving a bird, a plane, and a bear with that knife."

David also took up tool making at an early age. "When my parents' basketry tools broke," he says, "I'd fix them or make new ones. I got very involved in tool smithing and invented a lot of specialty tools." At age twelve, he invented a stand-up splint scraper, and over the years he has come up with other useful items such as an interchangeable gauge, a draw knife specially angled and designed for making basket handles and squaring off sticks of ash, and an interchangeable crooked knife that can be used by left- or right-handed crafters. At the moment, he's working on a small portable hydraulic pounder for preparing ash. He calls it "little big bear."

From the time he was born, David went with his family to work the blueberry harvest in Cherryfield each summer, and from ages fourteen to nineteen, he participated in part-time seasonal potato work. After graduating from Presque Isle High School in 1978, he earned his Class-II welder's license at Northern Maine Vocational Technical Institute. He worked as a structural welder at Loring Air Force Base in 1980. From 1981 to 1983 he worked as a carpenter, and from 1984 to 1985 as a carpet layer. In his spare time he made baskets, designed and made tools, and studied and eventually taught martial arts.

When he was fourteen, after two years of martial arts training, David took up training with a new teacher, James Black, a first-generation Japanese-American. "Jim was also a bladesmith," says David. "He'd learned to make swords from his grandfather and invited me to work with him. He's the one who taught me how to make Damascus steel, a mix of iron and steel. It's a precision process—folding the metals into each other exactly eighteen times while keeping them at a certain temperature." The result, a supremely strong as well as flexible metal, grabbed David's interest. "I'd watched my uncles forge crooked knife blades out of old files using the woodstove, no bellows. . . . When we used those knives a lot, the blades broke. So I started experimenting, looking for a way to make a stronger blade." James Black helped him find a way.

Karate had another important side effect for David. When he was eighteen, he met his wife, Janet Hutchings, at a karate school exhibition. "She was participating and I was watching," he says. "We got to know each other over the next few years and in 1983 we married." Janet, a computer operator for Maine Mutual Insurance, is neither a craftsperson nor a Micmac, but she is a strong supporter of her husband's work and heritage.

Three years ago David began working as a marketing consultant out of Presque Isle for Network Marketing, leaving him less time to spend on his crafts than he would like. "Right now my crafts are a hobby that I spend about ten hours a week on. I want to put more time into them because I really enjoy them." In addition to various tools, knives, and wood splint baskets, David has made and sold about thirty pairs of snowshoes. "My work is usually sold

64

before it's even made," he says. He also makes items for his own pleasure."I like to hunt traditionally with a handmade bow and arrow."

Of all his crafts, David most enjoys blacksmithing, appreciating the functionality and particularity of each knife. He pays as much attention to the handles as to the blades, carving them out of wood or antler. "Of all the knives I've made, no two are alike," he says. Building on the basic designs used by his uncle Wilfred, David customizes each knife to match his evolving taste and his customer's need. "I usually have the individual squeeze a hunk of clay and then carve the handle to match their grip," he says. David is not sure how many knives he's created since he made his first saleable crooked knife at age sixteen. He does remember receiving twenty dollars for that knife—considerably less than the $180 he gets for his best work today.

David and Janet have a daughter, Julia, who is four years old and a son, David, two. David hopes to pass his traditional crafts skills on to his children. In particular, he wants to show them basketry because it is "a unique chain in our family—something that's been passed down from every generation as far back as I know." David likes teaching Micmac traditions to other children as well, which he has done in his work as band president (1987) and youth coordinator (1988) for the Aroostook Micmac Council. "I'm especially interested in helping Micmac children be informed of and proud of their heritage, as I am."

David forging a crooked knife blade.

65

Roldena Sanipass is the third daughter of Donald and Mary Sanipass, two of the best-known basketmakers in Aroostook County today. She was born on September 21, 1966, in Ellsworth, Maine. Her parents had migrated to the area from Chapman (near Presque Isle) in August to rake blueberries, as they did every summer. "They stayed on a bit longer that year to work in the woods, and had me," says Roldena. Then they headed back to Aroostook to work the potato harvest and make baskets.

"I grew up with baskets," says Roldena. "I've played among the shavings since I was tiny." As soon as she was old enough, she joined her older sisters tucking splints, picking off loose splinters, sanding basket handles and hoops. When she was twelve, her brother David designed a stand-up splint shaver, a tool that made the task of scraping splints smooth far easier and safer than it was with a crooked knife. Using this, Roldena emerged as the family's chief splint shaver. But she rarely did the actual weaving. "Mom encouraged us to make baskets and I'd try occasionally, but I didn't see quality baskets coming from my hands like they did from Mom' s. So I ignored it for a while. At that point, basketry wasn't important to me and I didn't respect it as a profession. Guess I wasn't ready. Anyway, Mom didn't push me. She knew I had other things in life, so she let me go off on my own."

In l985 Roldena went to the University of Maine at Presque Isle. The following year she ventured south and worked in Portland as a dietary aid at a retirement home.

Roldena weaving a basket.

Roldena Sanipass
Chapman, Maine

There she met Lee Dudley, and in l987, "missing home," she brought him back to Aroostook. They moved in with Donald and Mary. "We were looking for a way to make a living," recollects Roldena. "Mom gave me some wood, showed me once how to make a round potato basket, and then I did it. I kept looking at it and I was very proud." Donald taught Lee how to select and prepare brown ash and how to make hoops and handles.

Roldena learned many "little secrets" from her mother. "She showed me how to curve the sides of a basket, how to use every finger, every muscle in your hands, how to mold baskets like pottery, how to use your instincts to feel the strength of the wood and know just how much you can pull and stretch it." Gradually, says Roldena, "I realized how much work and time you have to put into each basket. You put yourself into it and it becomes your baby, and you want it to work. Now, every basket I make is precious to me, like gold."

Today, basketry is a full-time livelihood for Roldena. She continues to work in partnership with Lee, making a wide variety of utility baskets and miniatures. They now have a daughter, "little Dena," and their own home in Chapman, about three miles from Donald and Mary. Their division of labor is very much like that of Donald and Mary who Roldena looks up to as role models. "I hope to follow in my parents' footsteps," she says, "continuing in this profession and getting better all the time. I don't want to give up basketry ever."

Roldena recognizes that, unlike her parents, she has taken up basketry at a time when hand-crafted goods are valued and increasingly rare. She enjoys giving demonstrations at

Roldena shouldering a stick of "basket ash" out of the woods.

67

fairs and schools, and has this to say about her work: "I'm proud to tell people I'm a basketmaker. Nowadays people look at you differently when you're good at this craft—with respect, the way they'd look at an endangered species." But perhaps most important to this young basketmaker is the way her mentors feel about her chosen profession. " I think Mom and Dad are as proud of me being a basketmaker as they'd be if I'd become a doctor."

The Collection
Photos by David Spahr

Potato baskets, listed by size: 17" wide x 11" deep, by Eldon Hanning; 16" wide x 8" deep, by Sarah Lund and Abe Harquail (not pictured); 12" wide x 5 $\frac{1}{4}$" deep, by Richard Silliboy; 11 $\frac{1}{4}$" wide x 6 $\frac{1}{2}$" deep, by Henry Lafford (deceased); 6 $\frac{1}{4}$" wide x 3 $\frac{1}{2}$" deep, by Roldena Sanipass; 4" wide x 2 $\frac{3}{4}$" deep, by Roldena Sanipass; **modified potato basket**, 9" wide x 10" deep, by Alex Harquail, son of Sarah Lund and Abe Harquail (not pictured).

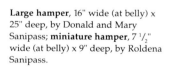

Large hamper, 16" wide (at belly) x
25" deep, by Donald and Mary
Sanipass; **miniature hamper**, 7 $\frac{1}{2}$"
wide (at belly) x 9" deep, by Roldena
Sanipass.

Round laundry basket, 17" wide x 18" deep, by Donald and Mary Sanipass; rectangular laundry basket, 29 $^1/_2$" long x 18 $^1/_2$" wide x 10 $^1/_2$" deep, by Ruby Schillinger.

Fishing creel, 10 $\frac{1}{2}$" long x 6 $\frac{1}{2}$" wide x 7 $\frac{1}{2}$" deep; **pack basket,** 14" wide (at belly) x 23" deep; **plain sewing basket** with lid, 7 $\frac{1}{2}$" wide x 6 $\frac{1}{2}$" deep—all three by Harold Lafford.

Small picnic basket, 10" square x 5 ¹/₂"
deep, by Harold Lafford; **large picnic
basket**, wrapped hoop, 18 ¹/₂" long x 13
¹/₄" wide x 8 " deep, by Joseph Silliboy;
handkerchief basket, 8" square x 4"
deep, by Harold Lafford; **round biscuit
basket**, 12 ¹/₂" wide x 4" deep, by Ruby
Schillinger.

Traditional-style fancy baskets are listed left-to-right: "**porcupine curlicue**" **jewelry basket** with lid and sweetgrass trim, 3" wide x 3" deep, by Jane Zumbrunnen; "**periwinkle curlicue**" **sewing basket** with lid and sweetgrass trim, 8" wide x 6" deep, by Jane Zumbrunnen; "**diamond curlicue**" **waste basket** with sweetgrass trim, 11" long x 8" wide x 11" deep, by Eldon Hanning; "**periwinkle curlicue**" **sewing basket** with lid, dyed splints and sweetgrass trim, 6 $^1/_2$" wide x 6" deep, by Jane Zumbrunnen; "**diamond curlicue**" **candy basket**, 4 $^1/_2$" wide x 3 $^1/_2$" deep, by Frank Hanning (Eldon's son); in center—"**diamond curlicue**" **handkerchief basket** with sweetgrass trim, 7" square x 3" deep, by Jane Zumbrunnen.

Nontraditional fancy sewing basket with lid, 9" long x 6" wide x 4" deep, by Alex Harquail (son of Sarah Lund and Abraham Harquail).

77

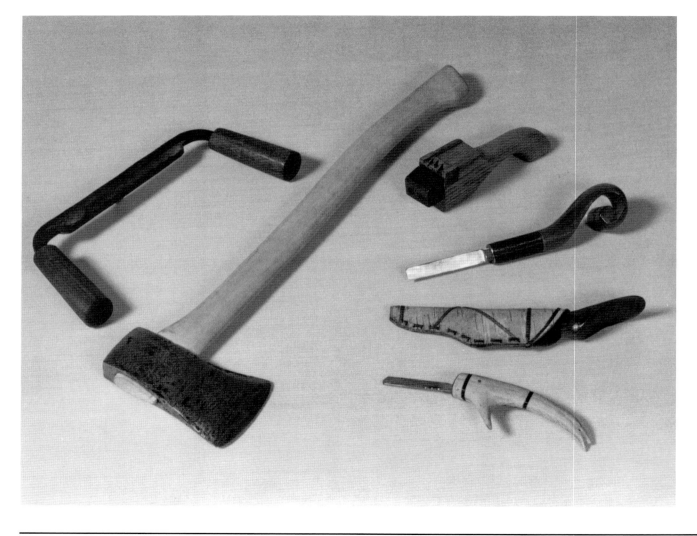

Basketry tools are listed clockwise: **draw shave knife with hand-carved mahogany handles and hand-forged layered steel blade**, by David Sanipass; **ax with hand-carved white ash handle**, by Wilfred Sanipass; **hand-carved red oak splint gauge** by David Sanipass; **crooked knife with birch handle**, hand-carved and forged by David Sanipass; **crooked knife with cherry handle and birchbark sheath**, by Wilfred Sanipass; **crooked knife with antler handle**, by David Sanipass. (Note: All three crooked knife blades are hand-forged from old files.)

78

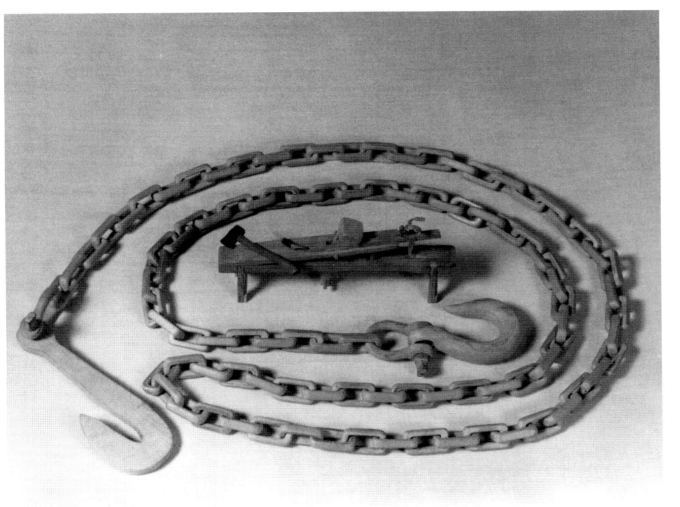

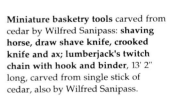

Miniature basketry tools carved from cedar by Wilfred Sanipass: **shaving horse, draw shave knife, crooked knife and ax; lumberjack's twitch chain with hook and binder**, 13' 2" long, carved from single stick of cedar, also by Wilfred Sanipass.

Shaving horse, pine and birch workbench with peddle clamp which holds wood in place while artisan carves it with a draw shave knife, by Wilfred Sanipass. Photo by Harald Prins.

Notes

1. *Our Lives in Our Hands*, © 1985 Carter and Prins, sponsored by the Aroostook Micmac Council, funded primarily by the Maine Humanities Council. The film may be rented from Documentary Educational Resources, Watertown, Massachusetts. Video copies may be purchased through Northeast Historic Film, Blue Hill, Maine.

2. Although other variations of the creation legend exist, this particular version is based on a tale published in M. Robertson, *Red Earth: Tales of the Micmacs with an Introduction to the Customs and Beliefs of the Micmac Indians*, Halifax: The Nova Scotia Museum, 1969, p. 27.

3. This interpretation of the Micmac tribal name is based on R. H. Whitehead, *Stories from the Six Worlds: Micmac Legends*, Halifax: Nimbus Publishing Ltd., 1988, p. 1.

4. An account of the Micmac way of life has been written by a French Jesuit missionary named Pierre Biard, active in Nova Scotia and Maine from 1611 to 1613. His work is titled "A Relation of New France, of its Lands, Nature of the Country, and of its Inhabitants (1616)," in R. G. Thwaites, ed., *The Jesuit Relations and Allied Documents*, vol. III, Cleveland: Burrows Brothers Company, 1897, pp. 79-83.

5. See E. T. Adney and H. I. Chapelle, *The Bark Canoe and Skin Boats of North America*, Washington, D.C: Smithsonian Institution, 1964, pp. 58-70; H. P. Beck, *The American Indian as a Sea-Fighter in Colonial Times*, Mystic, 1959, p. 13.

6. R. H. Whitehead, *Eliteky: Micmac Material Culture from 1600 A.D. to the Present*, Halifax: The Nova Scotia Museum, 1980, pp. 10-14. See also H. E. L. Prins and B. McBride, "A Social History of Maine Indian Basketry," in *Maine Basketry: Past to Present* (exhibit catalog), Waterville: Colby College Museum of Art, 1989, pp. 5-14.

7. Cited in W. D. Wallis and R. S. Wallis, *The Micmac Indians of Eastern Canada*, Minneapolis: University of Minnesota Press, 1955, pp.73-75.

8. N. Denys, *The Description and Natural History of the Coasts of North America (Acadia)*, Toronto: The Champlain Society, 1908, pp. 411-413. See also H. E. L. Prins, "Turmoil on the Wabanaki Frontier, 1524-1674," in R. Judd, ed., *The History of Maine*, Orono: University of Maine (forthcoming).

9. Wallis and Wallis, *op. cit.*, pp. 469-470.

10. Jacques Cartier, 1534, cited in M. Lescarbot, *The History of New France (1609-1612)*, Toronto: The Champlain Society, vol. II, p. 45. See also H. E. L. Prins and R. H. Whitehead, "A 16th-Century Micmac-Portuguese Pidgin in the Gulf of St. Lawrence," unpub. ms., 1986 (on file with authors).

11. See, among others, P. Biard, in Thwaites, *op. cit.*, vol. III, p.105; P. Bock, "Micmac," in B. G. Trigger, ed., *Handbook of North American Indians*, Washington, D.C.: Smithsonian Institution, 1978, vol. 15, p. 117.

12. P. Biard, Letter 1611, in Thwaites, ed., *op. cit.*, vol. II, p.177.

13. Denys, *op. cit.*, p. 444.

14. See also B. J. Bourque and R. H. Whitehead, "Tarrentines and the Introduction of European Tradegoods in the Gulf of Maine," in *Ethnohistory*, vol. 32, no. 4 (1986), pp. 327-341.

15. G. Archer, "The Relation of Captain Gosnold's Voyage to the North Part of Virginia, 1602," in *Collections of the Massachusetts Historical Society*, 3rd Series, vol. 8, Boston: Little Brown, 1843, pp. 73-74.

16. Among others, see Whitehead, *op. cit.*, 1980, p. 34.

17. H. E. L. Prins, *Tribulations of a Border Tribe: A Discourse on the Political Ecology of the Aroostook Band of Micmacs (16th-20th Centuries)*, Ann Arbor: University Microfilms International, 1988, pp. 212-216, 276-282.

18. A. de la Mothe Cadillac, "Memoire et Description de l'Acadie (1692)," (trans. and ed. by W. F. Ganong) in *Collections of the New Brunswick Historical Society*, no. 13, 1930, pp. 76-97.

19. H. E. L. Prins, "The Aroostook Band of Micmacs: An Historical Anthropological Review," in *Hearings before the Select Committee on Indian Affairs, United States Senate, 101st Congress, Report no. S1413*, Washington, D.C.: U.S. Government Printing Office (forthcoming), pp. 40-53.

20. Cited in *ibid.*, pp. 51-52.

21. Whitehead, *op. cit.*, 1980, p. 57.

22. S. T. Rand, *Dictionary of the Language of the Micmac Indians*,

81

Halifax: Nova Scotia Printing Company, 1888 (reissued by the Johnson Reprint Corporation, London, 1972).

23. Wallis and Wallis, *op. cit.*, pp. 7, 75.

24. T. J. Brasser, *A Basketful of Indian Culture Change*, National Museum of Man Mercury Series, Canadian Ethnology Service Paper no. 22, Ottawa: The National Museums of Canada, 1975, pp. 17-29.

25. Adney and Chapelle, *op. cit.*, p. 62.

26. Whitehead, *op. cit.*, 1980, pp. 54-58.

27. Among others, see L. F. S. Upton, *Micmacs and Colonists: Indian-White Relations in the Maritimes, 1713-1867*, Vancouver: University of British Columbia Press, 1979, pp. 128-129; E. Hutton, "Indian Affairs in Nova Scotia 1760-1834," in *Nova Scotia Historical Society Collections*, vol. 34, Halifax: Nova Scotia Historical Society, 1963, pp. 33-54.

28. Wallis and Wallis, *op. cit.*, p. 399.

29. Among others, see R. H. Whitehead, *Micmac Quillwork: Micmac Indian Techniques of Porcupine Quill Decoration: 1600-1950*, Halifax: The Nova Scotia Museum, 1982, pp. 66-71. See also F. H. Eckstorm, *The Handicrafts of the Modern Indians of Maine*, Bulletin III, Bar Harbor: Abbe Museum, 1932, pp.24-25. In addition, see *The Wabanakis of Maine and the Maritimes: A Resource Book about Penobscot, Passamaquoddy, Maliseet, Micmac and Abenaki Indians*, Philadelphia: American Friends Service Committee, 1989, pp. D-51, D-135.

30. Excerpts of a manuscript by John Glossian. See H. E. L. Prins, *The Micmac: Native Persistence and Cultural Survival*, New York: Holt Rinehart & Winston (work in progress).

31. *Ibid.*

32. R. J. Uniacke, *Sketches of Cape Breton and other Papers relating to Cape Breton Island (1865)*, Halifax: Public Archives of Nova Scotia, 1958, p. 108.

33. *Ibid.*

34. *Ibid.*, p. 107.

35. Whitehead, *op. cit.*, 1980, p. 55.

36. Brasser, *op. cit.*, pp 30-31; A. Bear Nicholas and H. E. L. Prins, "The Native People of Aroostook," in A. F. Mcgrath, ed., *The County: Land of Promise—A Pictorial History of Aroostook County*, *Maine*, Norfolk: The Donning Company, 1989, pp. 32-33.

37. H. E. L. Prins and B. McBride, Oral History of Caroline Sark Copage in *Genesis of the Micmac Community in Maine, and its Intricate Relationship to Micmac Reserves in the Maritimes*, Presque Isle: Aroostook Micmac Council Report, 1983 (on file with authors and Micmac Council).

38. Whitehead, *op. cit.*, 1982, p. 72.

39. *Ibid.*, p. 59.

40. See report by H. E. L. Prins, "Census and Vital Records of Maine Micmacs," 1985 (on file with author). For oral evidence, see oral history section of Prins and McBride, *op. cit.*, 1983.

41. H. E. L. Prins, "Review of A Key into the Language of Wood-splint Baskets," in *Pennsylvania Archaeologist*, vol. 58, no. 2 (1988), pp. 70-72.

42. Prins, *op. cit.*, 1988, pp. 70-72; Prins and McBride, *op. cit.* 1989, p. 12; see also Prins, *op. cit.*, 1985.

43. B. McBride, Interview with Dr. Ed Johnson, University of Maine, Orono, 1983 (on file with author); Prins and McBride, *op. cit.*, 1983, p. 72; see also G. F. DuBay, "The Garden of Maine," in Mcgrath, ed., *op. cit.*, pp. 152-160.

44. B. McBride, Interview with Larry Thibodeau, Maine Farmers' Exchange, Presque Isle, 1983 (on file with author).

45. B. McBride, "A Special Kind of Freedom," *Down East Magazine*, June, 1983.

46. B. McBride, Interview with Sarah Lund, Fort Kent, 1982 (on file with author).

47. Oral History of Sarah Lund, in Prins and McBride, *op. cit.*, 1983.

48. McBride, *op. cit.*, June, 1983.

49. B. McBride, Interview with Donald Sanipass, Chapman, 1990 (on file with author).

50. B. McBride, Interview with Richard Silliboy, 1989 (on file with author).

51. Quoted from *Our Lives in Our Hands* (the film), produced by K. Carter and H. E. L. Prins, 1985, distributed by Documentary Educational Resources, Watertown, Massachusetts, and Northeast Historic Film, Blue Hill, Maine.

52. McBride, *op. cit.*, June, 1983.

The **Micmac Basket Bank** is a nonprofit distribution center for Indian basketmakers. The sturdy baskets are made of hand-pounded brown ash. Each is signed by its Indian craftsperson, and comes with a tag describing the time-honored methods.

Because the baskets are completely handcrafted by individual basketmakers, they may vary a bit in size and detail, but high quality is consistent.

For more information or special orders, phone: 207-764-1972 or write: Aroostook Micmac Council Basket Bank, 8 Church Street, Presque Isle, Maine 04769.

Our Lives in Our Hands
Micmac Indian Basketmakers

Cover and text designed on Crummett Mountain by Edith Allard

Copyediting by Liz Pierson, South Harspwell, Maine

Layout by Nina Medina, Basil Hill Graphics, Coopers Mills, Maine

Editorial assistance by Janice Brackett

Imagesetting by High Resolutions, Inc., Camden, Maine

Printing and binding by Arcata Graphics, Kingsport, Tennessee